Taste *of* Home.
EVERYDAY
SHEET PAN

TASTE OF HOME BOOKS • RDA ENTHUSIAST BRANDS, LLC • MILWAUKEE, WI

Visit us at **tasteofhome.com** for other
Taste of Home books and products.

ISBN: 978-1-62145-529-5
LOCC: 2020949315

Executive Editor: Mark Hagen
Senior Art Director:
Raeann Thompson
Editor: Christine Rukavena
Assistant Art Director:
Courtney Lovetere
Designer: Jazmin Delgado
Deputy Editor, Copy Desk: Dulcie Shoener
Copy Editor: Sara Strauss

Cover:
Photographer: Dan Roberts
Set Stylist: Stacey Genaw
Food Stylist: Shannon Norris

Pictured on front cover:
Garlicky Chicken Dinner, p. 128

Pictured on spine:
Roasted Strawberry Sheet Cake, p. 242

Pictured on back cover:
Roasted Kielbasa & Vegetables, p. 151;
Baked Ham & Colby Sandwiches, p. 154;
Coconut-Macadamia Sheet-Pan Pancakes,
p. 21; Avocado Crab Boats, p. 192; Roast
Cauliflower with Pepperoncini, p. 75; Dad's
Favorite Barbecue Meat Loaves, p. 92

Printed in China

3 5 7 9 10 8 6 4 2

SUPER
CALZONES, P. 80

TABLE OF
CONTENTS

IIIIIIIIIIIIIIIIIIIIIIIIII

MORE WAYS TO CONNECT WITH US: f 𝕏 ⓘ ⓟ

FOR THE ULTIMATE IN WEEKNIGHT EASE,
GRAB YOUR SHEET PAN

Hearty, nutritious sheet-pan dinners are more popular than ever—and for good reason. The preparation is simple, the flavors are fresh and the cleanup is a breeze!

Inside **Taste of Home Everyday Sheet Pan,** you'll find 150 oven-fresh recipes—each a snap to prepare with ingredients you likely have in the kitchen already. Dig into dozens of busy-day favorites perfect for cozy meals as well as impressive menus ideal for weekend guests.

After all, easy dinners that bake hands-free are a joy on hectic nights. Try Tilapia with Corn Salsa (p. 180), for instance. It hits the table in just 10 minutes! You'll also find entire chapters for simply incredible beef entrees, convenient poultry dinners, juicy pork favorites and even meatless main courses.

Be sure to grab your baking pan for special occasions, too. Ginger-Cashew Chicken Salad (p. 119) is a sweet-tangy classic that is perfect for any gathering, and Orange-Glazed Pork with Sweet Potatoes (p. 159) is a lovely one-pan meal for holidays and other celebrations.

You'll also enjoy...

- Rise-and-shine specialties made on a sheet pan, including pancakes and one-dish bacon and eggs

- A Fast Fix icon 🕐 spotlighting 50 recipes ready in just 30 minutes or less

- More than a dozen sheet-pan party starters, so you always have hot and hearty munchies at the ready

- Sixteen tempting sweets that bake up beautifully every time

Today's cooks know that fabulous food doesn't have to be complicated. Streamline your dinner routine tonight with the finger-licking specialties in **Everyday Sheet Pan!**

SAUSAGE & PEPPER SHEET-PAN
SANDWICHES, P. 166

SELECTING A **SHEET PAN**

Sheet pans are among the most versatile tools you can find in the kitchen. Here are some tips to help you select the best sheet pans and to get the most from them. Then, start cooking up a few simple sheet-pan dinners of your own!

- Know the terminology. A sheet pan (called a 15x10x1-in. baking pan in our recipes) is a rimmed baking sheet. A baking (or cookie) sheet, on the other hand, does not have a rim. This gives you more surface area to fit on a few extra cookies, plus easy access to all parts of the baking sheet with a spatula.

- Sheet pans can stand in for cookie sheets, but it doesn't always work the other way around. The rolled edges of a sheet pan give you versatility because they catch juices, prevent spills and corral things like vegetables or meats for roasting.

- To find a sheet pan that will cook your food evenly and stand up to the abuse of a high-temperature oven, look for heavy-duty, warp-resistant pans.

- Heavy-gauge aluminum is a great option. It's one of our favorites for terrific heat conductivity, which helps produce nice browning. Tri-ply pans (so called because they're made of three fused layers of metal, often with an aluminum core) are another good option.

- It pays to spend a little more for quality. An inexpensive pan won't lay flat and has a tendency to warp in the oven. Not only that but its thin, flimsy material can easily cause the undersides of your food to burn.

- Nonstick pans are wonderful in the kitchen. But for roasting sheet-pan dinners (and making well-browned cookies), we recommend an uncoated metal surface. Nonstick can wear down and become scratched over time. It's also not safe for the broiler or other extreme temperatures—a versatility you might want when roasting your dinner.

- Once you find sheet pans you like, buy two at a time. That way you know they will cook ingredients and perform the same. And they'll nest together for easy storage.

BUILD A BETTER SHEET-PAN DINNER:

Sheet-pan dinners are a quick, easy way to put a healthy meal on the table. Follow these tips to whip up your own creation tonight.

- Invest in a good sheet pan
- Line the pan for easy cleanup
- Don't forget to toss the ingredients with a little oil first
- Season generously
- Don't overcrowd the pan
- Elevate the ingredients on an ovenproof wire cooling rack to crisp things up
- Give hearty vegetables (like potatoes or winter squash) a head start before adding other ingredients
- Rotate the pan halfway through cooking

ELEVATE INGREDIENTS FOR CRISPY RESULTS

THE RIM STOPS SPILLS

DON'T OVERCROWD

THESE SHEET-PAN IDEAS MAKE LIFE EASIER

Freezer Tray. A sheet pan makes it easy to freeze fresh fruit. Slice fruit if needed and place in a single layer on a sheet pan. Place the pan in the freezer and allow the fruit to freeze until solid. Remove, place in a freezer container, then return to the freezer until ready to use.

Oven Protector. There's nothing better than hot blueberry pie—unless it's bubbling all over the bottom of the oven because the juices overflowed. Slip a sheet pan on the bottom rack each time you bake a pie, lasagna or other dish that might bubble over, and you'll save yourself a messy chore. It's much easier to wash a pan than the floor of the oven.

Cutting Companion. If your cutting board doesn't have a rim, slicing juicy foods like pineapple or watermelon for fruit salad recipes can be tricky. To avoid juice dripping down the front of your cupboards, place a cutting board in a sheet pan before slicing. The sheet pan catches the excess juice and contains the mess. This also works when cutting the kernels off an ear of corn.

Pizza Pan. Cooking pizza on a preheated pizza stone makes it nice and crispy, but how do you get the pizza into and out of the oven? Flip a sheet pan over and use the back side to transfer the pizza without losing the toppings. If you don't

have a pizza stone, preheat an oiled sheet pan in the oven. Place pizza dough in the sheet pan and top with your favorite sauce and toppings. Cook until done, cool slightly, cut and serve.

Dish Carrier. A sheet pan is the perfect tool for loading and unloading individual ramekins into and out of the oven. It's also handy for transporting hot food or dishes that might spill on their way to a potluck. And how many times have you sloshed water out of the ice cube trays when carrying them from the sink to the freezer? Load them onto a sheet pan and then simply dump any excess water once you get the trays in the freezer.

HOW TO REVIVE A GRIMY SHEET PAN

GOT BAKED-ON GUNK? Here's how to make a sheet pan look brand-new. Whether you're whipping up a sheet-pan supper for the family or carefully crafting a gorgeous slab pie, a chef's sheet pan is likely to see plenty of wear and tear. Before you toss a favorite pan because of baked-on grime, try this easy way to clean and refresh it.

YOU'LL NEED:
- Baking soda
- Hydrogen peroxide
- Washcloth or scrubbing sponge

STEP 1: Apply the cleaning agents. Sprinkle some baking soda on the baking pan. Follow that with hydrogen peroxide and another sprinkling of baking soda. Let this mixture sit for at least two hours.

NOTE: Because this combination of soda and peroxide could be too harsh for some pans' materials or coatings, do a test run before cleaning an entire baking sheet, especially if it is made of a specialized material or has a coating of any kind.

STEP 2: Scrub away. Use a cloth or sponge to wipe away the homemade cleaner. Hard scrubbing usually isn't required. If stains remain, switch to a nonscratch scrubbing pad, try a second application of baking soda and hydrogen peroxide—or both. You just need a little patience!

STEP 3: Keep it clean. Now that your sheet pan is looking brand-new, consider lining it with parchment or aluminum foil before each use to keep it that way.

BREAKFAST
IN A PAN

||||||||||||||||||||

BREAKFAST
SWEET POTATOES

IIIIIIIIIIIIIIIIIIIIIIIIIIIIIIII

Baked sweet potatoes aren't just for dinner anymore. Top them with morning staples to power up your day.
—*Taste of Home* Test Kitchen

PREP: 10 MIN.
BAKE: 45 MIN.
MAKES: 4 SERVINGS

- 4 **medium sweet potatoes (about 8 oz. each)**
- ½ **cup fat-free coconut Greek yogurt**
- 1 **medium apple, chopped**
- 2 **Tbsp. maple syrup**
- ¼ **cup toasted unsweetened coconut flakes**

1. Preheat oven to 400°. Place potatoes on a foil-lined baking sheet. Bake until tender, 45-60 minutes.

2. With a sharp knife, cut an "X" in each potato. Fluff pulp with a fork. Top with remaining ingredients.

IIIIIIIIIIIIIIII

1 stuffed sweet potato: 321 cal., 3g fat (2g sat. fat), 0 chol., 36mg sod., 70g carb. (35g sugars, 8g fiber), 7g pro.

Test Kitchen Tip: Save time in the morning by baking and refrigerating the potatoes the night before. When it's time for breakfast, simply reheat the spuds in the microwave and top with the remaining ingredients.

MORNING BREAD BOWLS

||||||||||||||||||||||||||||||||||

These bread bowls are so elegant, tasty and simple, you'll wonder why you haven't been making them for years. My wife loves when I make these for her in the morning.
—Patrick Lavin Jr., Birdsboro, PA

PREP: 20 MIN.
BAKE: 20 MIN.
MAKES: 4 SERVINGS

- ½ cup chopped pancetta
- 4 crusty hard rolls (4 in. wide)
- ½ cup finely chopped fresh mushrooms
- 4 large eggs
- ⅛ tsp. salt
- ⅛ tsp. pepper
- ¼ cup shredded Gruyere or fontina cheese

1. Preheat oven to 350°. In a small skillet, cook pancetta over medium heat until browned, stirring occasionally. Remove with a slotted spoon; drain on paper towels.

2. Meanwhile, cut a thin slice off top of each roll. Hollow out bottom of roll, leaving a ½-in.-thick shell (save removed bread for another use); place shells on an ungreased baking sheet.

3. Add mushrooms and pancetta to bread shells. Carefully break an egg into each; sprinkle eggs with salt and pepper. Sprinkle with cheese. Bake 18-22 minutes or until the egg whites are completely set and yolks begin to thicken but are not hard.

|||||||||||||

1 breakfast bowl: 256 cal., 13g fat (5g sat. fat), 206mg chol., 658mg sod., 19g carb. (1g sugars, 1g fiber), 14g pro.

DELUXE HAM & EGG
SANDWICHES

|||||||||||||||||||||||||||||||||||

*My hearty cheesy breakfast
sandwiches are packed with
flavor. Between the layers of
cheese, I add ham, spinach
and eggs sunny side up.*
—Natalie Hess, Pennsville, NJ

TAKES: 30 MIN.
MAKES: 4 SERVINGS

- 1 **submarine bun, split**
- 4 **wedges The Laughing
  Cow garlic and herb
  Swiss cheese**
- 3 **oz. thinly sliced
  fully cooked
  Black Forest ham**
- 3 **tsp. butter, divided**
- ½ **medium red onion,
  thinly sliced**
- 2 **cups fresh baby spinach**
- 4 **large eggs**
- ⅛ **tsp. pepper**
- 4 **slices provolone cheese**

1. Preheat broiler. Cut bun crosswise in half; split each half to separate top and bottom. Spread with cheese wedges. Place on a foil-lined 15x10x1-in. baking pan.

2. Place a large nonstick skillet over medium-high heat; lightly brown ham on each side. Place ham on bread.

3. In same skillet, heat 1 tsp. butter over medium-high heat. Add onion and spinach; cook and stir 2-4 minutes or until spinach is wilted. Divide mixture among sandwiches. Wipe skillet clean if necessary.

4. In same skillet, heat remaining butter over medium-high heat. Break eggs and slip into pan, 1 at a time. Immediately reduce heat to low; cover and cook slowly 5-6 minutes or until egg whites are completely set and yolks begin to thicken but are not hard. Sprinkle with pepper.

5. Place eggs over the spinach mixture; top with provolone cheese. Broil 4-5 in. from heat 2-3 minutes or until cheese is slightly melted.

|||||||||||||

*1 open-faced sandwich: 293 cal., 17g fat (9g sat. fat),
223mg chol., 768mg sod., 14g carb. (4g sugars, 1g fiber),
20g pro.*

RASPBERRY
BREAKFAST BRAID

||||||||||||||||||||||||||||||||||||||

We like using blackberries, Marionberries or a mixture of both in this quick, easy pastry.
—Tressa Nicholls, Sandy, OR

PREP: 20 MIN.
BAKE: 15 MIN.
MAKES: 12 SERVINGS

- 2 cups biscuit/baking mix
- 3 oz. cream cheese, cubed
- ¼ cup cold butter, cubed
- ⅓ cup 2% milk
- 1¼ cups fresh raspberries
- 3 Tbsp. sugar
- ¼ cup vanilla frosting

1. Preheat oven to 425°. Place biscuit mix in a large bowl. Cut in cream cheese and butter until mixture resembles coarse crumbs. Stir in milk just until moistened. Turn onto a lightly floured surface; knead gently 8-10 times.

2. On a greased baking sheet, roll dough into an 18x12-in. rectangle. Spoon raspberries down center third of dough; sprinkle with sugar.

3. On each long side, cut 1-in.-wide strips about 2½ in. into center. Starting at 1 end, fold alternating strips at an angle across raspberries; seal ends.

4. Bake until golden brown, 15-20 minutes. Remove to a wire rack to cool slightly. In a microwave-safe dish, microwave frosting on high until it reaches desired consistency, 5-10 seconds; drizzle over pastry.

||||||||||||

1 slice: 185 cal., 10g fat (5g sat. fat), 19mg chol., 319mg sod., 22g carb. (8g sugars, 1g fiber), 2g pro.

PECAN
BACON

IIIIIIIIIIIIIIIIIIIIIIIIIIIIIIIIIII

Crispy, sweet bacon brightens up any morning. When my girls see this, they call it "special breakfast." The big flavor punch may just surprise you.
—Catherine Ann Goza, Charlotte, NC

PREP: 10 MIN.
BAKE: 25 MIN.
MAKES: 1 DOZEN

 12 bacon strips
 ¼ cup packed brown sugar
 ¼ cup finely chopped
      pecans
 ⅛ tsp. ground cinnamon
 ⅛ tsp. pepper

1. Preheat oven to 375°. Place bacon in a single layer in a foil-lined 15x10x1-in. baking pan. Bake until lightly browned, 16-18 minutes.

2. Remove bacon from pan. Discard drippings from pan, wiping clean if necessary.

3. In a shallow bowl, mix remaining ingredients. Dip both sides of bacon in brown sugar mixture, patting to help coating adhere; return to pan.

4. Bake until caramelized, 8-10 minutes longer. Remove immediately from pan.

IIIIIIIIIIIII

1 bacon strip: 142 cal., 12g fat (4g sat. fat), 18mg chol., 186mg sod., 4g carb. (4g sugars, 0 fiber), 4g pro.

SMOKED SAUSAGE
BREAKFAST HASH

||||||||||||||||||||||||||||||||||

This hash, full of red potatoes, sweet potatoes and sausage, brightens up any day. Spread the love throughout the week by piling leftovers into burritos and casseroles.
—Jamie Burton, Highlands Ranch, CO

PREP: 15 MIN.
BAKE: 25 MIN.
MAKES: 4 SERVINGS

- 1 lb. red potatoes (about 3 medium), cut into ½-in. cubes
- 1 medium sweet potato, peeled and cut into ½-in. cubes
- 1 medium onion, chopped
- 1½ cups sliced smoked turkey sausage (about 8 oz.)
- 4 garlic cloves, minced
- 1 tsp. Creole seasoning
- 2 cups chopped fresh spinach
- 1 Tbsp. butter
- 4 large eggs

1. Preheat oven to 425°. In a large bowl, toss together the first 6 ingredients. Spread evenly in a greased 15x10x1-in. baking pan. Roast 20-25 minutes or until vegetables are tender, stirring once. Stir in spinach; roast 5 minutes longer.

2. Meanwhile, in a large nonstick skillet, heat butter over medium-high heat. Break eggs, 1 at a time, into pan; immediately reduce heat to low. Cook until whites are completely set and yolks begin to thicken but are not hard, about 5 minutes. Serve over hash.

||||||||||||||

1 egg with 1¼ cups hash: 317 cal., 11g fat (4g sat. fat), 229mg chol., 842mg sod., 35g carb. (8g sugars, 4g fiber), 19g pro.

GARLIC-HERB
MINI QUICHES

|||||||||||||||||||||||||||||||||||||||

Looking for a wonderful little bite to dress up a brunch buffet? These delectable tartlets are irresistible!
—Josephine Piro, Easton, PA

TAKES: 25 MIN.
MAKES: 45 MINI QUICHES

1 pkg. (6½ oz.) reduced-fat garlic-herb spreadable cheese
¼ cup fat-free milk
2 large eggs
3 pkg. (1.9 oz. each) frozen miniature phyllo tart shells
2 Tbsp. minced fresh parsley
   Minced chives, optional

1. In a small bowl, beat the spreadable cheese, milk and eggs. Place tart shells on an ungreased baking sheet; fill each with 2 tsp. mixture. Sprinkle with parsley.

2. Bake at 350° for 10-12 minutes or until filling is set and shells are lightly browned. Sprinkle with chives if desired. Serve warm.

|||||||||||||

1 mini quiche: 31 cal., 2g fat (0 sat. fat), 12mg chol., 32mg sod., 2g carb. (0 sugars, 0 fiber), 1g pro.

COCONUT-MACADAMIA
SHEET-PAN PANCAKES

IIIIIIIIIIIIIIIIIIIIIIIIIIIIIIIIIII

These are great for brunch when you want to serve a group without standing over the stove. The fun flavors give this dish a tropical flair. Try pineapple-flavored ice cream topping instead of the usual maple syrup.
—Trisha Kruse, Eagle, ID

PREP: 15 MIN. + STANDING
BAKE: 15 MIN.
MAKES: 10 SERVINGS

3½ cups complete
     buttermilk pancake mix
½ cup sweetened
     shredded coconut
2 cups 2% milk
1 Tbsp. coconut oil or
     butter, softened
½ cup macadamia nuts,
     coarsely chopped
2 medium bananas, sliced
     Butter and maple syrup

1. Preheat oven to 425°. In a large bowl, combine the pancake mix and shredded coconut. Stir in milk just until the dry ingredients are moistened; let stand 10 minutes. Meanwhile, line a 15x10x1-in. baking pan with parchment; grease parchment with coconut oil.

2. Spread batter into prepared pan; sprinkle with macadamia nuts. Bake until puffy and golden brown, 15-20 minutes. Cool in pan on a wire rack 5 minutes. Carefully lift parchment to remove from pan. Top with sliced bananas; serve with butter and syrup.

IIIIIIIIIIII

1 piece: 288 cal., 11g fat (4g sat. fat), 4mg chol., 642mg sod., 44g carb. (13g sugars, 2g fiber), 7g pro.

SHEET-PAN
BACON & EGGS BREAKFAST

||||||||||||||||||||||||||||||||

I re-created this recipe from something I saw on social media, and it was a huge hit! Use any cheeses and spices you like—you can even try seasoned potatoes.
—Bonnie Hawkins, Elkhorn, WI

PREP: 20 MIN.
BAKE: 40 MIN.
MAKES: 8 SERVINGS

- 10 bacon strips
- 1 pkg. (30 oz.) frozen shredded hash brown potatoes, thawed
- 1 tsp. garlic powder
- 1 tsp. dried basil
- 1 tsp. dried oregano
- ½ tsp. salt
- ½ tsp. crushed red pepper flakes
- 1½ cups shredded pepper jack cheese
- 1 cup shredded cheddar cheese
- ¼ tsp. pepper
- 8 large eggs
- ¼ cup chopped green onions

1. Preheat oven to 400°. Place the bacon in a single layer in a 15x10x1-in. baking sheet. Bake until partially cooked but not crisp, about 10 minutes. Remove to paper towels to drain. When cool enough to handle, chop bacon; set aside.

2. In a large bowl, combine the potatoes and seasonings; spread evenly into drippings in pan. Bake until golden brown, 25-30 minutes.

3. Sprinkle with cheeses. With the back of a spoon, make 8 wells in potato mixture. Break an egg in each well; sprinkle with pepper and reserved bacon. Bake until egg whites are completely set and yolks begin to thicken but are not hard, 12-14 minutes. Sprinkle with green onions.

|||||||||||||

1 serving: 446 cal., 30g fat (13g sat. fat), 246mg chol., 695mg sod., 22g carb. (2g sugars, 1g fiber), 22g pro.

SMOKED SALMON &
EGG WRAPS

IIIIIIIIIIIIIIIIIIIIIIIIIIIIIIIIIII

*These quick roll-ups are ideal
when you're serving a morning
crowd. Everyone enjoys the
smoked salmon flavor, which is
nicely accented by a hint of dill
in the eggs.*
—Mary Lou Wayman, Salt Lake City, UT

TAKES: 25 MIN.
MAKES: 10 SERVINGS

- 12 **large eggs**
- ¼ **cup snipped fresh dill
   or 4 tsp. dill weed**
- 2 **Tbsp. 2% milk**
- ½ **tsp. seasoned salt**
- 10 **flour tortillas (8 in.)**
- 1 **pkg. (4 oz.) smoked
   salmon or lox**
- ½ **cup finely chopped
   red onion**
- 6 **oz. Havarti cheese,
   thinly sliced**

1. In a large bowl, whisk the eggs, dill, milk and seasoned salt. Coat a large skillet with cooking spray and place over medium heat. Add egg mixture. Cook and stir over medium heat until eggs are completely set.

2. Spoon a scant ⅓ cup egg mixture down the center of each tortilla. Top with salmon, onion and cheese. Fold opposite sides of tortilla over filling (the sides will not meet in center). Roll up tortilla, beginning at 1 of the open ends. Place the wraps, seam side down, in a 15x10x1-in. baking pan coated with cooking spray.

3. Cover and bake at 350° for 10 minutes or until the cheese is melted.

IIIIIIIIIIIIII

1 serving: 314 cal., 15g fat (6g sat. fat), 273mg chol., 733mg sod., 27g carb. (1g sugars, 0 fiber), 18g pro.

PORTOBELLO MUSHROOMS
FLORENTINE

||||||||||||||||||||||||||||||||||||||

This fast and fun idea is packed with flavor. What a rich, hearty take on stuffed mushrooms, particularly for breakfast.
—Sara Morris, Laguna Beach, CA

TAKES: 25 MIN.
MAKES: 2 SERVINGS

- 2 **large portobello mushrooms, stems removed**
  Cooking spray
- ⅛ **tsp. garlic salt**
- ⅛ **tsp. pepper**
- ½ **tsp. olive oil**
- 1 **small onion, chopped**
- 1 **cup fresh baby spinach**
- 2 **large eggs**
- ⅛ **tsp. salt**
- ¼ **cup crumbled goat or feta cheese**
  Minced fresh basil, optional

1. Preheat oven to 425°. Spritz mushrooms with cooking spray; place in a 15x10x1-in. pan, stem side up. Sprinkle with garlic salt and pepper. Bake, uncovered, until tender, about 10 minutes.

2. Meanwhile, in a nonstick skillet, heat oil over medium-high heat; saute onion until tender. Stir in spinach until wilted.

3. Whisk together eggs and salt; add to skillet. Cook and stir until eggs are thickened and no liquid egg remains; spoon onto mushrooms. Sprinkle with cheese and, if desired, basil.

||||||||||||||

1 stuffed mushroom: 126 cal., 5g fat (2g sat. fat), 18mg chol., 472mg sod., 10g carb. (4g sugars, 3g fiber), 11g pro. Diabetic exchanges: 2 vegetable, 1 lean meat, ½ fat.

Health Tip: At about 30 calories and 4 grams carbs per cap, portobello mushrooms are a low-cal, low-carb way to serve up eggs. Try filling with other combos like cooked sausage, sauce and mozzarella; feta, basil and tomatoes; or quinoa, garbanzos and goat cheese.

ALMOND-CHAI
GRANOLA

||||||||||||||||||||||||||||||||||

Whether you snack on it by the handful or eat it with milk or yogurt, you'll be happy that you made this granola.
—Rachel Preus, Marshall, MI

PREP: 20 MIN.
BAKE: 1¼ HOURS + COOLING.
MAKES: 8 CUPS

- 2 **chai tea bags**
- ¼ **cup boiling water**
- 3 **cups quick-cooking oats**
- 2 **cups almonds, coarsely chopped**
- 1 **cup sweetened shredded coconut**
- ½ **cup honey**
- ¼ **cup olive oil**
- ⅓ **cup sugar**
- 2 **tsp. vanilla extract**
- ¾ **tsp. salt**
- ¾ **tsp. ground cinnamon**
- ¾ **tsp. ground nutmeg**
- ¼ **tsp. ground cardamom**

1. Preheat oven to 250°. Steep tea bags in boiling water 5 minutes. Meanwhile, combine oats, almonds and coconut. Discard tea bags; stir remaining ingredients into tea. Pour tea mixture over oat mixture; mix well to coat.

2. Spread mixture evenly in a greased 15x10x1-in. pan. Bake until golden brown, stirring every 20 minutes, about 1¼ hours. Cool completely without stirring; store in an airtight container.

|||||||||||||

½ cup: 272 cal., 16g fat (3g sat. fat), 0 chol., 130mg sod., 29g carb. (16g sugars, 4g fiber), 6g pro. Diabetic exchanges: 3 fat, 2 starch.

BREAKFAST SAUSAGE BREAD

IIIIIIIIIIIIIIIIIIIIIIIIIIIIIII

Any time we take this savory, satisfying bread to a brunch, it goes over very well. We never bring any home. My husband usually makes it, and he prides himself on how beautifully the golden loaves bake.
—Shirley Caldwell, Northwood, OH

PREP: 25 MIN. + RISING
BAKE: 25 MIN.
MAKES: 2 LOAVES
(16 SLICES EACH)

- 2 loaves (1 lb. each) frozen white bread dough, thawed
- ½ lb. mild pork sausage
- ½ lb. bulk spicy pork sausage
- 1½ cups diced fresh mushrooms
- ½ cup chopped onion
- 3 large eggs, divided use
- 2½ cups shredded mozzarella cheese
- 1 tsp. dried basil
- 1 tsp. dried parsley flakes
- 1 tsp. dried rosemary, crushed
- 1 tsp. garlic powder

1. Cover dough and let rise in a warm place until doubled. Preheat oven to 350°. In a large skillet, cook the sausage, mushrooms and onion over medium-high heat until sausage is no longer pink, breaking sausage into crumbles, 6-8 minutes. Drain. Transfer to a bowl; cool.

2. Stir in 2 eggs, cheese and seasonings. Roll each loaf of dough into a 16x12-in. rectangle. Spread half of the sausage mixture over each rectangle to within 1 in. of edges. Roll up jelly-roll style, starting with a short side; pinch seams to seal. Place on a greased baking sheet.

3. In a small bowl, whisk remaining egg. Brush over tops. Bake until golden brown, 25-30 minutes. Serve warm.

FREEZE OPTION: Securely wrap and freeze cooled loaves in foil and place in resealable plastic freezer bags. To use, place foil-wrapped loaf on a baking sheet and reheat in a 450° oven until heated through, 10-15 minutes. Carefully remove foil; return to oven a few minutes longer until crust is crisp.

IIIIIIIIIIII

1 slice: 102 cal., 6g fat (2g sat. fat), 32mg chol., 176mg sod., 8g carb. (1g sugars, 1g fiber), 5g pro.

READER REVIEW
"Excellent recipe! It reheats nicely. It turned out to be a great Christmas morning tradition. It is also good with a side of warm marinara sauce for dipping."
—SHORTCAKETOO, TASTEOFHOME.COM

SHEET-PAN
SNACKS

||||||||||||||||||||

GREEN CHILE
PROSCIUTTO
ROLLS

IIIIIIIIIIIIIIIIIIIIIIIIIIIIIIII

I created these for my husband, who loves green chiles. He likes these rolls so much he could eat a whole pan.
—Paula McHargue, Richmond, KY

TAKES: 25 MIN.
MAKES: 14

- 1   tube (8 oz.) refrigerated crescent rolls
- 3   oz. cream cheese, softened
- 1   can (4 oz.) chopped green chiles, drained
- 1   Tbsp. sweet hot mustard
- ½   cup thinly sliced prosciutto, cooked and crumbled
- 1   large egg, beaten
- 3   Tbsp. grated Parmesan cheese

1. Preheat oven to 375°. Unroll crescent dough into 1 long rectangle; press perforations to seal. In a small bowl, beat cream cheese, green chiles and mustard. Spread over dough to within ½ in. of edges. Sprinkle with prosciutto. Roll up the left and right sides toward the center, jelly-roll style, until rolls meet in the middle. Cut into 1-in. slices.

2. Place cut side up on a parchment-lined baking sheet. Brush with egg; sprinkle with Parmesan cheese. Bake until golden brown, 12-15 minutes. If desired, top with additional grated Parmesan cheese.

IIIIIIIIIIII

1 roll: 98 cal., 6g fat (2g sat. fat), 23mg chol., 258mg sod., 8g carb. (2g sugars, 0 fiber), 3g pro.

APPLE-GOUDA
PIGS IN A BLANKET

||||||||||||||||||||||||||||||||||||||||

For New Year's, I used to make beef and cheddar pigs in a blanket, but now I like this apple and Gouda filling even better.
—Megan Weiss, Menomonie, WI

TAKES: 30 MIN.
MAKES: 2 DOZEN

1 **tube (8 oz.) refrigerated crescent rolls**
1 **small apple, peeled and cut into 24 thin slices**
6 **thin slices Gouda cheese, quartered**
24 **miniature smoked sausages**
   Honey mustard salad dressing, optional

1. Preheat oven to 375°. Unroll crescent dough and separate into 8 triangles; cut each lengthwise into 3 thin triangles. On the wide end of each triangle, place 1 slice apple, 1 folded piece cheese and 1 sausage; roll up tightly.

2. Place 1 in. apart on parchment-lined baking sheets, point side down. Bake until golden brown, 10-12 minutes. If desired, serve with dressing.

||||||||||||||

1 appetizer: 82 cal., 6g fat (2g sat. fat), 11mg chol., 203mg sod., 5g carb. (1g sugars, 0 fiber), 3g pro.

TASTY
TOMATO
PIZZA

||||||||||||||||||||||||||||||||||

I'm known for bringing this party-style pizza everywhere I go. It's an easy bite when you use refrigerated dough and a big baking pan.
—Kim Evarts, Brockport, NY

PREP: 20 MIN.
BAKE: 20 MIN.
MAKES: 24 PIECES

- 1 tube (13.8 oz.) refrigerated pizza crust
- ⅔ cup mayonnaise
- ⅓ cup grated Parmesan cheese
- 1 Tbsp. minced fresh basil or 1 tsp. dried basil
- ½ tsp. garlic powder
- ½ tsp. garlic salt
- 2 cups shredded part-skim mozzarella cheese, divided
- 5 plum tomatoes (about 1½ lbs.), cut into ¼-in. slices
- 1 can (2¼ oz.) sliced ripe olives, drained
- ¼ cup chopped green pepper, optional

1. Preheat oven to 375°. Unroll and press dough onto bottom and ½ in. up sides of a greased 15x10x1-in. baking pan.

2. In a small bowl, combine mayonnaise, Parmesan cheese, basil, garlic powder and garlic salt. Stir in 1½ cups mozzarella cheese. Spread over crust. Top with tomato slices, olives and, if desired, green pepper. Sprinkle with remaining cheese.

3. Bake 20-25 minutes or until crust is golden brown and cheese is melted.

||||||||||||

1 piece: 123 cal., 8g fat (2g sat. fat), 9mg chol., 276mg sod., 9g carb. (2g sugars, 1g fiber), 4g pro.

SWEET & SPICY
JALAPENO POPPERS

|||||||||||||||||||||||||||||||||||

*There's no faster way to get a
party started than with these
bacon-wrapped poppers. Make
them ahead and bake just
before serving.*
—Dawn Onuffer, Crestview, FL

TAKES: 30 MIN.
MAKES: 1 DOZEN

- 6 jalapeno peppers
- 4 oz. cream cheese,
  softened
- 2 Tbsp. shredded cheddar
  cheese
- 6 bacon strips, halved
  widthwise
- ¼ cup packed brown sugar
- 1 Tbsp. chili seasoning
  mix

1. Cut jalapenos in half lengthwise and remove seeds; set aside.
In a small bowl, beat cheeses until blended. Spoon into pepper
halves. Wrap a half-strip of bacon around each pepper half.

2. Combine brown sugar and chili seasoning; coat peppers with
sugar mixture. Place in a greased 15x10x1-in. baking pan.

3. Bake at 350° until bacon is firm, 18-20 minutes.

NOTE: Wear disposable gloves when cutting hot peppers; the oils
can burn your skin. Avoid touching your face.

||||||||||||

*1 stuffed pepper half: 66 cal., 5g fat (3g sat. fat), 15mg
chol., 115mg sod., 3g carb. (3g sugars, 0 fiber), 2g pro.*

READER REVIEW
*"These are always a win! When
I don't feel like dealing with the
jalapenos or I want to bring a less
spicy option, I use mini sweet
peppers instead. They're a totally
different flavor but still really good!"*
—GINA.KAPFHAMER, TASTEOFHOME.COM

NACHO TRIANGLES WITH
SALSA-RANCH DIPPING SAUCE

||||||||||||||||||||||||||||||||

*These nacho bites are a fun
fusion of Greek appetizers
and flavors of the American
Southwest. The simple dipping
sauce is a perfect match—the
ranch balances out the heat
of the jalapeno and chipotle
peppers—and takes the recipe
to the next level.*

—Angela Spengler, Niceville, FL

PREP: 45 MIN.
BAKE: 15 MIN.BATCH
MAKES: 4 DOZEN

- ½ **lb. ground beef**
- ¼ **cup finely chopped onion**
- ½ **cup shredded pepper
  jack cheese**
- ½ **cup shredded cheddar
  cheese**
- ¼ **cup frozen corn, thawed**
- ¼ **cup canned diced
  tomatoes**
- 2 **Tbsp. taco seasoning**
- 2 **Tbsp. finely chopped
  seeded jalapeno pepper**
- 1 **Tbsp. finely chopped
  chipotle peppers in
  adobo sauce**
- 32 **sheets phyllo dough
  (14x9-in. size)**
- ¾ **cup butter, melted**
- ½ **cup ranch salad
  dressing**
- ½ **cup salsa**

1. Preheat oven to 375°. In a small skillet, cook beef and onion over medium heat until the beef is no longer pink and onion is tender, 5-7 minutes, breaking up beef into crumbles; drain. Stir in cheeses, corn, tomatoes, taco seasoning, jalapeno and the chipotle pepper; set aside.

2. Place 1 sheet phyllo dough on a work surface; brush lightly with butter. Cover with another sheet of phyllo; brush with butter. (Keep remaining phyllo covered with a damp towel to prevent it from drying out.)

3. Cut the 2 layered sheets into three 14x3-in. strips. Place 1 Tbsp. filling about 1 in. from the corner of each strip. Fold 1 corner of dough over filling, forming a triangle. Fold triangle over, forming another triangle. Continue folding, like a flag, until you reach the end of the strip. Brush end of dough with butter and press onto triangle to seal. Turn triangle and brush top with butter. Repeat with remaining phyllo and filling.

4. Place triangles on greased baking sheets. Bake until golden brown, 12-15 minutes. Combine ranch dressing and salsa; serve with triangles.

FREEZE OPTION: Freeze cooled triangles in freezer containers. To use, reheat the triangles on a greased baking sheet in a preheated 375° oven until crisp and heated through.

||||||||||||

1 appetizer: 77 cal., 5g fat (3g sat. fat), 13mg chol., 143mg sod., 5g carb. (1g sugars, 0 fiber), 2g pro.

ROASTED BRUSSELS SPROUTS
WITH SRIRACHA AIOLI

||||||||||||||||||||||||||||||||||||||

This dish constantly surprises. It's crispy, easy to eat, totally sharable and yet, it is a vegetable! This recipe is also gluten-free, dairy-free and paleo, and it can also be vegan if you use vegan mayo.
—Molly Winsten, Brookline, MA

PREP: 20 MIN.
COOK: 20 MINUTES
MAKES: 8 SERVINGS

- 1 lb. fresh Brussels sprouts, trimmed and halved
- 2 Tbsp. olive oil
- 2 to 4 tsp. Sriracha chili sauce, divided
- ½ tsp. salt, divided
- ½ tsp. pepper, divided
- ½ cup mayonnaise
- 2 tsp. lime juice
- 1 Tbsp. lemon juice

1. Preheat oven to 425°. Place Brussels sprouts on a rimmed baking sheet. Drizzle with oil and 1 tsp. Sriracha chili sauce; sprinkle with ¼ tsp. salt and ¼ tsp. pepper. Toss to coat. Roast until crispy, about 20-25 minutes.

2. Meanwhile, mix mayonnaise, lime juice, remaining 1-3 tsp. Sriracha chili sauce, ¼ tsp. salt and ¼ tsp. pepper. Drizzle lemon juice over Brussels sprouts before serving with sauce.

|||||||||||||

4 halves with 1 Tbsp. sauce: 146 cal., 14g fat (2g sat. fat), 1mg chol., 310mg sod., 6g carb. (2g sugars, 2g fiber), 2g pro.

Take It Down a Notch: *Not keen on red-hot spice? Simply reduce the Sriracha chili sauce to ¼ tsp.*

STUFFED
ASIAGO-BASIL
MUSHROOMS

||||||||||||||||||||||||||||||||||

Even if you don't care for mushrooms, you will have to give these tasty appetizers a try! They're divine. For a main dish, simply double the filling and use large portobellos.
—Lorraine Caland, Shuniah, ON

PREP: 25 MIN.
BAKE: 10 MIN.
MAKES: 2 DOZEN

- 24 **baby portobello mushrooms (about 1 lb.), stems removed**
- ½ **cup reduced-fat mayonnaise**
- ¾ **cup shredded Asiago cheese**
- ½ **cup loosely packed basil leaves, stems removed**
- ¼ **tsp. white pepper**
- 12 **cherry tomatoes, halved**
  Thinly sliced or shaved Parmesan cheese, optional

1. Preheat oven to 375°. Place mushroom caps in a greased 15x10x1-in. baking pan. Bake 10 minutes. Meanwhile, place mayonnaise, Asiago cheese, basil and pepper in a food processor; process until blended.

2. Drain juices from mushrooms. Fill each with 1 rounded tsp. mayonnaise mixture; top each with a tomato half.

3. Bake 8-10 minutes or until lightly browned. If desired, top with Parmesan cheese.

||||||||||||

1 appetizer: 35 cal., 3g fat (1g sat. fat), 5mg chol., 50mg sod., 2g carb. (1g sugars, 0 fiber), 2g pro.

Italian Sausage Mushrooms: *Omit filling. Bake and drain mushroom caps as directed. In a large skillet, cook 1 pound bulk Italian sausage over medium heat until no longer pink; drain. In a bowl, mix 6 oz. softened cream cheese, 3 Tbsp. minced fresh parsley and the sausage; spoon into mushroom caps. Bake as directed. Sprinkle with an additional 1 Tbsp. minced fresh parsley.*

WARM SPICED NUTS

||||||||||||||||||||||||||||||||||||||

I like to set out bowls of spiced nuts when hosting holiday parties. They bake up so easily on a sheet pan. Sometimes I stir M&M's into the cooled nut mixture for an addictive sweet and salty snack.

—Jill Matson, Zimmerman, MN

PREP: 5 MIN.
BAKE: 30 MIN.
MAKES: 3 CUPS

- 1   cup pecan halves
- 1   cup unblanched almonds
- 1   cup unsalted dry roasted peanuts
- 3   Tbsp. butter, melted
- 4½ tsp. Worcestershire sauce
- 1   tsp. chili powder
- ½   tsp. garlic salt
- ¼   tsp. cayenne pepper

1. In a large bowl, combine the pecans, almonds and peanuts. Combine butter and Worcestershire sauce; pour over nuts and toss to coat.

2. Spread in a single layer in an ungreased 15x10x1-in. baking pan. Bake at 300° until browned, about 30 minutes, stirring occasionally.

3. Transfer warm nuts to a bowl. Combine the chili powder, garlic salt and cayenne; sprinkle over nuts and stir to coat. Serve the nuts warm, or allow to cool before storing in an airtight container.

|||||||||||||

¼ cup: 231 cal., 22g fat (4g sat. fat), 8mg chol., 123mg sod., 7g carb. (2g sugars, 3g fiber), 6g pro.

HAM BALLS WITH
BROWN SUGAR GLAZE

IIIIIIIIIIIIIIIIIIIIIIIIIIIIIIIIII

These smoky-sweet meatballs are a Pennsylvania Dutch specialty. I like setting them out when folks come to visit.
—Janet Zeger, Middletown, PA

PREP: 30 MIN.
BAKE: 30 MIN.
MAKES: ABOUT 6 DOZEN

- 1 lb. fully cooked ham, cubed
- 1 lb. ground pork
- 1 cup 2% milk
- 1 cup crushed cornflakes
- 1 large egg, lightly beaten
- ¼ cup packed brown sugar
- 1 Tbsp. ground mustard
- ½ tsp. salt

GLAZE
- 1 cup packed brown sugar
- ¼ cup vinegar
- 1 Tbsp. ground mustard

1. Preheat oven to 350°. Pulse ham in batches in a food processor until finely ground. Combine with the next 7 ingredients just until mixed. Shape into 1-in. balls; place in a single layer on greased 15x10x1-in. baking pans.

2. For glaze, cook and stir all ingredients in a small saucepan over medium heat until sugar is dissolved. Spoon over ham balls. Bake 30-35 minutes or until ham balls are just beginning to brown, rotating pans and carefully stirring halfway through. Gently toss in glaze. Serve warm.

IIIIIIIIIIIII

1 meatball: 52 cal., 2g fat (1g sat. fat), 11mg chol., 113mg sod., 5g carb. (4g sugars, 0 fiber), 3g pro.

SAVORY CRACKER
SNACK MIX

||||||||||||||||||||||||||||||||||

*Because I love the seasonings
on Everything Bagels, I decided
to give this a try. It's a regular
snack at my home.*
—Cyndy Gerken, Naples, FL

PREP: 15 MIN.
BAKE: 15 MIN. + COOLING
MAKES: 4½ CUPS

- 1½ cups potato sticks
- 1½ cups cheddar-flavored
  snack crackers
- 1½ cups sourdough pretzel
  nuggets
- 3 Tbsp. butter
- ¼ cup grated Parmesan
  cheese
- 3 Tbsp. olive oil
- 1½ tsp. sesame seeds
- 1½ tsp. dried minced garlic
- 1½ tsp. dried minced onion
- 1½ tsp. poppy seeds
- ¼ tsp. kosher salt

1. Preheat oven to 350°. In a large bowl, combine potato sticks, crackers and pretzels. In a small saucepan, melt butter; stir in the remaining ingredients. Drizzle over the pretzel mixture; toss to coat.

2. Spread in a greased 15x10x1-in. baking pan. Bake until crisp and lightly browned, 12-15 minutes, stirring every 4 minutes. Cool completely in pan on a wire rack. Store snack mix in an airtight container.

||||||||||||||

¾ cup: 306 cal., 20g fat (7g sat. fat), 20mg chol., 468mg sod., 26g carb. (1g sugars, 1g fiber), 5g pro.

Get Creative: *Feel free to swap the snack crackers with oyster crackers. Or toss in a handful of nuts. You can also experiment with herbs and seasonings. Make it your own!*

SWISS CHERRY
BRUSCHETTA

||||||||||||||||||||||||||||||||||

This recipe is a take on a cherry chicken main dish my husband adores. The combination of sweet, tart and salty flavors provides a contrast that's hard to resist.
—Shelly Platten, Amherst, WI

TAKES: 30 MIN.
MAKES: 16 SERVINGS

- 2 **large onions, chopped**
- 1 **garlic clove, minced**
- 4 **tsp. olive oil**
- 1 **Tbsp. balsamic vinegar**
- 1 **tsp. brown sugar**
- ½ **tsp. garlic salt**
- 2½ **cups pitted dark sweet cherries, coarsely chopped**
- 16 **slices French bread (½ in. thick), lightly toasted**
- 1½ **cups shredded Swiss cheese**
- 2 **Tbsp. minced fresh parsley**

1. In a large skillet, saute onions and garlic in oil until tender, about 6 minutes. Add the vinegar, brown sugar and garlic salt; reduce heat. Cook until onions are caramelized, 3-4 minutes. Stir in the cherries; cook until the sauce is syrupy, about 5 minutes longer.

2. Place toasted bread on a baking sheet; spoon cherry mixture evenly over toast. Sprinkle with the cheese and parsley. Broil 3-4 in. from the heat until cheese is melted, 1-2 minutes.

|||||||||||||

1 serving: 115 cal., 4 g fat (2 g sat. fat), 9 mg chol., 154 mg sod., 15 g carb., 1 g fiber, 4 g pro.

OVEN-FRIED
PICKLES

||||||||||||||||||||||||||||||||||||||

*Like deep-fried pickles? You'll
love this un-fried version even
more. I coat pickle slices with
panko bread crumbs then bake
them on a baking sheet until
crispy. Dip the slices in ranch
dressing for an appetizer you
won't forget.*
—Nick Iverson, Denver, CO

PREP: 20 MIN. + STANDING
BAKE: 20 MIN.
MAKES: 8 SERVINGS

- 32 dill pickle slices
- ½ cup all-purpose flour
- ½ tsp. salt
- 2 large eggs, lightly beaten
- 2 Tbsp. dill pickle juice
- ½ tsp. cayenne pepper
- ½ tsp. garlic powder
- ½ cup panko bread crumbs
- 1 Tbsp. snipped fresh dill

1. Preheat oven to 500°. Let pickle slices stand on a paper towel until liquid is almost absorbed, about 15 minutes.

2. Meanwhile, in a shallow bowl, combine flour and salt. In another shallow bowl, whisk eggs, pickle juice, cayenne and garlic powder. Combine panko and dill in a third shallow bowl.

3. Dip pickles in flour mixture to coat both sides; shake off excess. Dip in egg mixture, then in crumb mixture, patting to help coating adhere. Transfer to a greased wire rack in a rimmed baking sheet.

4. Bake until golden brown and crispy, 20-25 minutes.

|||||||||||||

4 pickle slices: 65 cal., 2g fat (0 sat. fat), 47mg chol.,421mg sod., 9g carb. (1g sugars, 1g fiber), 3g pro.

ISLAND CHICKEN WINGS

||||||||||||||||||||||||||||||||||

These baked chicken wings are a tasty twist on regular wings. The orange flavor is a game-changer and will have you coming back for seconds!
—Caren Berry, Lancaster, CA

PREP: 35 MIN.
BAKE: 40 MIN.
MAKES: 3 DOZEN

18 chicken wings
    (about 3½ lbs.)
1   can (12 oz.) frozen
    orange juice
    concentrate, thawed
3   cups flaked coconut
3   cups panko bread
    crumbs
3   Tbsp. grated orange
    zest
1   Tbsp. minced fresh
    gingerroot
1   tsp. curry powder
½   tsp. salt
¼   tsp. pepper
1   cup orange marmalade
3   Tbsp. hot water
¼ to ½ tsp. crushed
    red pepper flakes

1. Preheat oven to 350°. Line a 15x10x1-in. baking pan with foil and coat with cooking spray; set aside.

2. Cut wings into 3 sections; discard wing tip sections. Place orange juice concentrate in a shallow bowl. In a separate shallow bowl, combine the coconut, bread crumbs, orange zest, ginger, curry powder, salt and pepper. Dip chicken wings in orange juice concentrate then coat with coconut mixture.

3. Place on prepared baking sheet. Bake until the juices run clear, 40-50 minutes. Meanwhile, in a small bowl, combine the marmalade, hot water and pepper flakes. Serve with wings.

|||||||||||||

1 wing: 128 cal., 6g fat (3g sat. fat), 14mg chol., 81mg sod., 14g carb. (10g sugars, 1g fiber), 5g pro.

SWIFT &
SAVORY
SIDES

|||||||||||||||||||

BUTTERNUT SQUASH
PANZANELLA SALAD

||||||||||||||||||||||||||||||||

This salad is easy to make, and it's even easier if you use precut chunks of butternut squash. You can use pecans in place of the almonds or watercress instead of arugula.
—Nancy Buchanan, Costa Mesa, CA

PREP: 25 MIN.
BAKE: 20 MIN.
MAKES: 8 SERVINGS

- 6 cups cubed day-old French bread (bite-sized cubes)
- 3 Tbsp. olive oil
- ½ tsp. chili powder
- ¼ tsp. salt

SALAD
- 4 cups cubed peeled butternut squash (1½-in. cubes)
- 1½ cups sliced fresh mushrooms
- ½ cup olive oil, divided
- ½ tsp. salt, divided
- ½ tsp. pepper, divided
- 6 cups fresh arugula or fresh baby spinach
- 6 Tbsp. sherry vinegar
- 3 shallots, thinly sliced
- ½ cup salted roasted almonds
- 6 Tbsp. crumbled goat cheese

1. Preheat oven to 400°. Toss bread cubes with oil, chili powder and salt. Spread evenly in an ungreased 15x10x1-in. baking pan. Bake until golden brown, about 5 minutes. Transfer to a large bowl; cool.

2. In another large bowl, combine squash and mushrooms. Add 2 Tbsp. oil, ¼ tsp. salt and ¼ tsp. pepper; toss to coat. Transfer to a greased 15x10x1-in. baking pan. Roast until tender, 20-25 minutes, stirring occasionally.

3. Add arugula and squash mixture to toasted bread. In a small bowl, whisk together vinegar, shallots and remaining oil, salt and pepper. Drizzle over salad; toss gently to combine. Top with almonds and goat cheese. Serve immediately.

||||||||||||

¾ cup: 361 cal., 26g fat (4g sat. fat), 7mg chol., 435mg sod., 29g carb. (5g sugars, 4g fiber), 7g pro.

READER REVIEW
"I added dried cranberries and candied pecans instead of the walnuts. The roasted butternut squash, along with the goat cheese and arugula, were not only pretty, but absolutely delicious. Will definitely make again!"
—DEBGLASS11, TASTEOFHOME.COM

CURRIED SWEET POTATO WEDGES

||||||||||||||||||||||||||||||||

Sweet potatoes roasted with curry and smoked paprika delight everybody. The mango chutney makes a tangy dip.
—Simi Jois, Streamwood, IL

TAKES: 25 MIN.
MAKES: 4 SERVINGS

- 2   medium sweet potatoes (about 1 lb.), cut into ½-in. wedges
- 2   Tbsp. olive oil
- 1   tsp. curry powder
- ½   tsp. salt
- ½   tsp. smoked paprika
- ⅛   tsp. coarsely ground pepper
      Minced fresh cilantro
      Mango chutney, optional

1. Preheat oven to 425°. Place sweet potatoes in a large bowl. Mix oil and seasonings; drizzle over sweet potatoes and toss to coat. Transfer to an ungreased 15x10x1-in. baking pan.

2. Roast 15-20 minutes or until tender, turning occasionally. Sprinkle with cilantro. If desired, serve with chutney.

||||||||||||

1 serving: 159 cal., 7g fat (1g sat. fat), 0 chol., 305mg sod., 23g carb. (9g sugars, 3g fiber), 2g pro. Diabetic exchanges: 1½ starch, 1½ fat.

SPINACH SALAD WITH
RASPBERRIES & CANDIED WALNUTS

||||||||||||||||||||||||||||||||||||

I created a bright spinach salad with raspberries for a big family dinner, and the festive colors fit right in with the holiday table. Even those who don't like spinach change their minds at the very first bite.
—Robert Aucelluzzo, Simi Valley, CA

PREP: 15 MIN.
BAKE: 25 MIN. + COOLING
MAKES: 8 SERVINGS

  1 **large egg white**
  ¾ **tsp. vanilla extract**
  2 **cups walnut halves**
  ½ **cup sugar**

DRESSING
  ¼ **cup canola oil**
  2 **Tbsp. cider vinegar**
  1 **Tbsp. sugar**
 1½ **tsp. light corn syrup**
  1 **tsp. poppy seeds**
  ¼ **tsp. salt**
  ¼ **tsp. ground mustard**

SALAD
  8 **oz. fresh baby spinach (about 10 cups)**
 1½ **cups fresh raspberries**

1. Preheat oven to 300°. In a small bowl, whisk egg white and vanilla until frothy. Stir in walnuts. Sprinkle with sugar; toss to coat evenly. Spread in a single layer in a greased 15x10x1-in. baking pan.

2. Bake 25-30 minutes or until lightly browned, stirring every 10 minutes. Spread on waxed paper to cool completely.

3. In a small bowl, whisk dressing ingredients until blended. Place spinach in a large bowl. Drizzle with dressing; toss to coat. Sprinkle with raspberries and 1 cup candied walnuts (save remaining walnuts for another use).

||||||||||||||

1½ cups: 171 cal., 13g fat (1g sat. fat), 0 chol., 100mg sod., 12g carb. (9g sugars, 3g fiber), 3g pro. Diabetic exchanges: 1½ fat, 1 starch, 1 vegetable.

ROASTED RED
POTATO SALAD

||||||||||||||||||||||||||||||||||

I got this recipe from my sister-in-law and I've made it numerous times at the request of friends. It's quick and easy, which is just what I need in my busy life. I learned how to cook from the two best cooks I know, my mom and my grandma.

—Ginger Cusano, Sandusky, OH

PREP: 40 MIN. + CHILLING
MAKES: 8 SERVINGS

- 2 lbs. red potatoes, cut into 1-in. cubes
- 1 medium onion, chopped
- 4 hard-boiled large eggs, sliced
- 6 bacon strips, cooked and crumbled
- 1 cup mayonnaise
- ½ tsp. salt
- ¼ tsp. pepper
   Paprika and minced fresh parsley, optional

1. Place the potatoes in a greased 15x10x1-in. baking pan. Bake, uncovered, at 400° until tender and golden brown, stirring occasionally, 25-30 minutes. Cool for 15 minutes.

2. Transfer to a large bowl; add onion, eggs, bacon, mayonnaise, salt and pepper. Toss to coat. Cover and refrigerate for several hours or overnight. If desired, sprinkle with the paprika and minced parsley.

|||||||||||||

¾ cup: 355 cal., 27g fat (5g sat. fat), 120mg chol., 412mg sod., 20g carb. (3g sugars, 2g fiber), 7g pro.

A Bit of Tenderness: When roasting potatoes, don't just rely on the bake time in the recipe. If they're not tender, then keep on cooking.

SOUR CREAM &
CHEDDAR
BISCUITS

||||||||||||||||||||||||||||||||||

*Here's my go-to recipe for
biscuits. Brushing them with
the garlic-butter topping before
baking seals the deal!*
—Amy Martin, Vancouver, WA

PREP: 25 MIN.
BAKE: 15 MIN.
MAKES: 1½ DOZEN

2½ cups all-purpose flour
3 tsp. baking powder
2 tsp. sugar
1 tsp. garlic powder
½ tsp. cream of tartar
¼ tsp. salt
¼ tsp. cayenne pepper
½ cup cold butter, cubed
1½ cups shredded cheddar
    cheese
¾ cup 2% milk
½ cup sour cream

TOPPING
6 Tbsp. butter, melted
1½ tsp. garlic powder
1 tsp. minced fresh
    parsley

1. Preheat oven to 450°. In a bowl, whisk the first 7 ingredients. Cut in cold butter until mixture resembles coarse crumbs; stir in cheese. Add milk and sour cream; stir just until moistened.

2. Drop by ¼ cupfuls 2 in. apart onto greased baking sheets. Mix topping ingredients; brush over the tops. Bake 12-15 minutes or until light brown. Serve warm.

|||||||||||||

1 biscuit: 206 cal., 14g fat (8g sat. fat), 36mg chol., 256mg sod., 15g carb. (2g sugars, 1g fiber), 5g pro.

GARLIC-ROASTED BRUSSELS SPROUTS
WITH MUSTARD SAUCE

IIIIIIIIIIIIIIIIIIIIIIIIIIIIIIIIIII

Don't be afraid to bring out the Brussels sprouts. Mellowed by roasting and tossed with mustard sauce, they may just delight even the most skeptical folks at your table.
—Becky Walch, Orland, CA

TAKES: 20 MIN.
MAKES: 6 SERVINGS

1½ lbs. fresh Brussels
    sprouts, halved
2 Tbsp. olive oil
3 garlic cloves, minced
½ cup heavy whipping
    cream
3 Tbsp. Dijon mustard
⅛ tsp. white pepper
    Dash salt

1. Place Brussels sprouts in an ungreased 15x10x1-in. baking pan. Combine olive oil and minced garlic; drizzle over sprouts and toss to coat.

2. Bake sprouts, uncovered, at 450° until tender, 10-15 minutes, stirring occasionally.

3. Meanwhile, in a small saucepan, combine the cream, mustard, pepper and salt. Bring to a gentle boil; cook until slightly thickened, 1-2 minutes. Spoon over Brussels sprouts.

IIIIIIIIIIIII

¾ cup: 167 cal., 12g fat (5g sat. fat), 27mg chol., 241mg sod., 13g carb. (3g sugars, 4g fiber), 4g pro.

ROASTED SWEET POTATOES
WITH DIJON
& ROSEMARY

||||||||||||||||||||||||||||||||||

*After moving to Alabama,
I learned my co-workers and
friends love sweet potatoes.
I roast these potatoes with
Dijon, fresh rosemary and
a touch of honey.*
—Tamara Huron, New Market, AL

PREP: 10 MIN.
BAKE: 25 MIN.
MAKES: 4 SERVINGS

- 2   **medium sweet potatoes
    (about 1½ lbs.)**
- 2   **Tbsp. olive oil**
- 2   **tsp. Dijon mustard**
- 2   **tsp. honey**
- 1   **tsp. minced fresh
    rosemary or ¼ tsp. dried
    rosemary, crushed**
- ¼   **tsp. salt**
- ¼   **tsp. pepper**

Preheat oven to 400°. Peel and cut each sweet potato lengthwise into ½-in.-thick wedges; place in a large bowl. Mix remaining ingredients; drizzle over potatoes and toss to coat. Transfer to a greased 15x10x1-in. baking pan. Roast 25-30 minutes or until tender, stirring occasionally.

|||||||||||||

1 serving: 170 cal., 7g fat (1g sat. fat), 0 chol., 217mg sod., 26g carb. (12g sugars, 3g fiber), 2g pro. Diabetic exchanges: 2 starch, 1½ fat.

LEMON-PARMESAN
BROILED ASPARAGUS

||||||||||||||||||||||||||||

These spears are packed with flavor, thanks to the lemon-garlic dressing they're tossed in before roasting. It's a simple, quick side that goes with almost anything!
—Tina Mirilovich, Johnstown, PA

TAKES: 15 MIN.
MAKES: 4 SERVINGS

¼   cup mayonnaise
4   tsp. olive oil
1½ tsp. grated lemon zest
1   garlic clove, minced
½   tsp. pepper
¼   tsp. seasoned salt
1   lb. fresh asparagus, trimmed
2   Tbsp. shredded Parmesan cheese
    Lemon wedges, optional

1. Preheat broiler. In large bowl, combine the first 6 ingredients. Add asparagus; toss to coat. Place in a single layer on a wire rack over a foil-lined 15x10x1-in. baking pan.

2. Broil 5-6 in. from heat until tender and lightly browned, 5-7 minutes. Transfer to a serving platter; sprinkle with Parmesan cheese. If desired, serve with lemon wedges.

|||||||||||||

1 serving: 156 cal., 15g fat (3g sat. fat), 3mg chol., 309mg sod., 3g carb. (1g sugars, 1g fiber), 2g pro. Diabetic exchanges: 3 fat, 1 vegetable.

Keeping Asparagus Fresh: To keep asparagus fresh longer, place the cut stems in a container of cold water—similar to flowers in a vase. Place the container in the refrigerator, changing the water at least once every 2 days.

GOUDA & ROASTED
POTATO BREAD

||||||||||||||||||||||||||||||||||||

Our family tried roasted potato bread at a bakery on a road trip, and I came up with my own recipe when we realized we lived much too far away to have it regularly. It makes for a really amazing roast beef sandwich and is also great with soups.
—Elisabeth Larsen, Pleasant Grove, UT

PREP: 45 MIN. + RISING
BAKE: 40 MIN.
MAKES: 1 LOAF (16 SLICES)

- ½ lb. Yukon Gold potatoes, chopped (about ¾ cup)
- 1½ tsp. olive oil
- 1½ tsp. salt, divided
- 1 pkg. (¼ oz.) active dry yeast
- 2½ to 3 cups all-purpose flour
- 1 cup warm water (120° to 130°)
- ½ cup shredded smoked Gouda cheese

1. Arrange 1 oven rack at lowest rack setting; place second rack in middle of oven. Preheat oven to 425°. Place potatoes in a greased 15x10x1-in. baking pan. Drizzle with oil; sprinkle with ½ tsp. salt. Toss to coat. Roast until tender, 20-25 minutes, stirring occasionally.

2. In a large bowl, mix yeast, remaining 1 tsp. salt and 2 cups flour. Add warm water; beat on medium speed until smooth. Stir in enough remaining flour to form a soft dough (dough will be sticky). Turn dough onto a floured surface; knead until smooth and elastic, 6-8 minutes. Gently knead in roasted potatoes and cheese. Place in a greased bowl, turning once to grease the top. Cover and let rise in a warm place until doubled, about 1 hour.

3. Punch down dough. Shape into a 7-in. round loaf. Place on a parchment-lined baking sheet. Cover with a kitchen towel; let rise in a warm place until dough expands to a 9-in. loaf, about 45 minutes.

4. Place an oven-safe skillet on bottom oven rack. Meanwhile, in a teakettle, bring 2 cups water to a boil. Using a sharp knife, make a slash (¼ in. deep) across top of loaf. Place bread on top rack. Pull bottom rack out by 6-8 in.; add boiling water to skillet. (Work quickly and carefully, pouring water away from you. Don't worry if some water is left in the kettle.) Carefully slide bottom rack back into place; quickly close door to trap steam in oven.

5. Bake 10 minutes. Reduce oven setting to 375°. Bake until deep golden brown, 30-35 minutes longer. Remove loaf to a wire rack to cool.

||||||||||||||

1 slice: 101 cal., 2g fat (1g sat. fat), 4mg chol., 253mg sod., 18g carb. (0 sugars, 1g fiber), 3g pro.

TUSCAN-STYLE
ROASTED ASPARAGUS

IIIIIIIIIIIIIIIIIIIIIIIIIIIIIII

This is especially wonderful when locally grown asparagus is in season . It's so easy for celebrations because you can serve it hot or cold.
—Jannine Fisk, Malden, MA

PREP: 20 MIN.
BAKE: 15 MIN.
MAKES: 8 SERVINGS

1½ lbs. fresh asparagus, trimmed
1½ cups grape tomatoes, halved
3 Tbsp. pine nuts
3 Tbsp. olive oil, divided
2 garlic cloves, minced
1 tsp. kosher salt
½ tsp. pepper
1 Tbsp. lemon juice
⅓ cup grated Parmesan cheese
1 tsp. grated lemon zest

1. Preheat oven to 400°. Place the asparagus, tomatoes and pine nuts on a foil-lined 15x10x1-in. baking pan. Mix 2 Tbsp. oil, garlic, salt and pepper; add to asparagus and toss to coat.

2. Bake 15-20 minutes or just until asparagus is tender. Drizzle with remaining oil and the lemon juice; sprinkle with cheese and lemon zest. Toss to combine.

IIIIIIIIIIIII

1 serving: 95 cal., 8g fat (2g sat. fat), 3mg chol., 294mg sod., 4g carb. (2g sugars, 1g fiber), 3g pro. Diabetic exchanges: 1½ fat, 1 vegetable.

Choosing the Right Oil: Common olive oil works better for cooking at high heat than virgin or extra virgin oil. These higher grades have ideal flavor for cold foods, but they smoke at lower temperatures.

GINGER BEETS
& CARROTS

||||||||||||||||||||||||||||||||||||

I love fresh garden foods, especially those as hearty as beets and carrots. This is a delicious way to enjoy a farmers market haul. The ginger adds both flavor and health benefits.
—Courtney Stultz, Weir, KS

TAKES: 25 MIN.
MAKES: 4 SERVINGS

- 1½ cups thinly sliced fresh carrots
- 1½ cups thinly sliced fresh beets
- 4 tsp. olive oil
- 1½ tsp. honey
- 1½ tsp. ground ginger
- ¾ tsp. soy sauce
- ½ tsp. sea salt
- ½ tsp. chili powder

Preheat oven to 400°. Place the vegetables in a greased 15x10x1-in. baking pan. Whisk remaining ingredients; drizzle over vegetables. Toss to coat. Bake until carrots and beets are crisp-tender, 15-20 minutes.

|||||||||||||||

½ cup: 92 cal., 5g fat (1g sat. fat), 0 chol., 379mg sod., 12g carb. (8g sugars, 3g fiber), 1g pro. Diabetic exchanges: 1 starch, 1 vegetable.

READER REVIEW
"I turned this into a sheet-pan dinner by adding chicken breasts and adjusting the baking time until the chicken was cooked through."
—MARYANNET, TASTEOFHOME.COM

ROASTED ARTICHOKES
WITH LEMON AIOLI

||||||||||||||||||||||||||||||||

*Petals of savory artichoke
leaves are so delicious dipped
into a creamy lemon aioli. It
may seem intimidating to roast
whole artichokes, but the steps
couldn't be simpler—and the
earthy, comforting flavor is a
definite payoff.*
—*Taste of Home* Test Kitchen

PREP: 20 MIN.
BAKE: 50 MIN.
MAKES: 4 SERVINGS

    4   medium artichokes
    2   Tbsp. olive oil
    ½   medium lemon
    ½   tsp. salt
    ¼   tsp. pepper

AIOLI
    ¼   cup mayonnaise
    ¼   cup plain Greek yogurt
    ½   tsp. minced fresh garlic
    ¼   tsp. grated lemon zest
        Dash pepper

1. Preheat oven to 400°. Using a sharp knife, cut 1 in. from top
of each artichoke. Using kitchen scissors, cut off tips of outer
leaves. Cut each artichoke lengthwise in half. With a spoon,
carefully scrape and remove fuzzy center of artichokes.

2. Drizzle oil into a 15x10x1-in. baking pan. Rub cut surfaces of
artichokes with lemon half; sprinkle with salt and pepper. Place
in pan, cut side down. Squeeze lemon juice over artichokes.
Cover pan with foil; bake on a lower oven rack until tender and
a leaf near the center pulls out easily, 50-55 minutes.

3. Meanwhile, mix aioli ingredients; refrigerate until serving.
Serve with artichokes.

||||||||||||||

*2 halves with 2 Tbsp. aioli: 233 cal., 19g fat (3g sat. fat),
5mg chol., 446mg sod., 16g carb. (2g sugars, 7g fiber),
4g pro.*

CHIPOTLE SWEET POTATO SALAD

||||||||||||||||||||||||||||||||||

I love the velvety taste and texture of sweet potatoes. A friend served sweet potatoes cooked with peppers and they tasted delicious together. I took those flavors and developed them into this creamy, smoky potato salad.

—Carolyn Eskew, Dayton, OH

PREP: 20 MIN.
BAKE: 25 MIN. + COOLING
MAKES: 9 SERVINGS

- 3 lbs. sweet potatoes, peeled and cut into ¾-in. pieces (about 7 cups)
- ¼ cup finely chopped sweet onion
- ¼ cup finely chopped celery
- ¼ cup finely chopped seeded fresh poblano pepper
- 1 jalapeno pepper, seeded and finely chopped
- 1 cup mayonnaise
- 2 Tbsp. lime juice
- ½ to 1 tsp. ground chipotle pepper
- ½ tsp. salt
- ¼ tsp. pepper
  Minced fresh cilantro

1. Preheat oven to 425°. Place sweet potatoes in a parchment-lined 15x10x1-in. baking pan; cover tightly with foil. Roast until tender, 25-30 minutes. Cool. Transfer to a large bowl.

2. Add onion, celery, poblano and jalapeno. Combine the mayonnaise, lime juice, chipotle pepper, salt and pepper; pour over potato mixture and toss gently to coat. Refrigerate, covered, until serving. Sprinkle with cilantro.

|||||||||||||

¾ cup: 322 cal., 18g fat (3g sat. fat), 2mg chol., 278mg sod., 38g carb. (16g sugars, 5g fiber), 3g pro.

Chill Out: If you're going to refrigerate this salad for more than a couple of hours before serving, stir in just half of the dressing mixture. Add the rest right before dinner for a nice creamy texture.

ROAST CAULIFLOWER WITH
PEPPERONCINI

||||||||||||||||||||||||||||||||||

I never enjoyed cauliflower until I found this recipe. I tweaked the dish for many years and finally found this perfect mix of flavors and ingredients.
—Hannah Hicks, Marina del Rey, CA

TAKES: 30 MIN.
MAKES: 6 SERVINGS

- 1 **large head cauliflower, broken into florets (about 8 cups)**
- 1 **Tbsp. plus 1 tsp. olive oil, divided**
- ¼ **tsp. kosher salt**
- ¼ **tsp. pepper**
- 1 **jar (3½ oz.) capers, drained and patted dry**
- 1 **jar (16 oz.) pepperoncini, drained and coarsely chopped**
- ½ **cup sliced almonds, toasted**
- 1 **Tbsp. sherry vinegar**

1. Preheat oven to 450°. Place cauliflower in a 15x10x1-in. baking pan. Drizzle with 1 Tbsp. oil; sprinkle with salt and pepper. Roast until tender, 15-20 minutes, stirring halfway through bake time.

2. Meanwhile, in a small skillet, heat remaining 1 tsp. oil over medium-high heat. Add capers; cook and stir until golden brown, 4-6 minutes. Drain on paper towels.

3. Stir pepperoncini, almonds and capers into cauliflower; drizzle with vinegar. Serve immediately.

||||||||||||||

¾ cup: 122 cal., 7g fat (1g sat. fat), 0 chol., 962mg sod., 11g carb. (3g sugars, 4g fiber), 5g pro.

Simple Swap: If you cannot find sherry vinegar, red wine vinegar works just as well.

ROASTED
BEET
WEDGES

|||||||||||||||||||||||||||||||||||

This recipe makes ordinary beets taste tender and delicious with just a few good-for-you ingredients.
—Wendy Stenman, Germantown, WI

PREP: 15 MIN.
BAKE: 1 HOUR
MAKES: 4 SERVINGS

1 **lb. medium fresh beets, peeled**
4 **tsp. olive oil**
½ **tsp. kosher salt**
3 **to 5 fresh rosemary sprigs**

1. Preheat oven to 400°. Cut each beet into 6 wedges; place in a shallow dish. Add olive oil and salt; toss gently to coat.

2. Place a piece of heavy-duty foil 12 in. long in a 15x10x1-in. baking pan. Arrange beets on foil; top with rosemary. Fold foil around beets and seal tightly.

3. Bake until tender, about 1 hour. Open foil carefully to allow steam to escape. Discard rosemary sprigs.

||||||||||||||

3 wedges: 92 cal., 5g fat (1g sat. fat), 0 chol., 328mg sod., 12g carb. (9g sugars, 3g fiber), 2g pro. Diabetic exchanges: 1 vegetable, 1 fat.

Time Saver: *You may make the beets a day ahead, then slice and serve cold in a salad.*

MEXICAN ROASTED
POTATO SALAD

||||||||||||||||||||||||||||||||||||||

My husband doesn't like potato salad, but he loves this one! It makes a fabulous side dish for grilled chicken or burgers. I usually serve it warm, but the leftovers are truly outstanding straight from the fridge.
—Elisabeth Larsen, Pleasant Grove, UT

PREP: 20 MIN.
BAKE: 25 MIN.
MAKES: 10 SERVINGS

- 4 lbs. potatoes, peeled and cut into ½-in. cubes (about 8 cups)
- 1 Tbsp. canola oil
- 1½ tsp. salt, divided
- ½ tsp. pepper
- 1 can (15 oz.) black beans, rinsed and drained
- 1 can (4 oz.) chopped green chiles
- 2 Tbsp. minced fresh cilantro
- ¾ cup sour cream
- ¾ cup mayonnaise
- 2 tsp. lime juice
- 1 tsp. ground chipotle pepper or 2 tsp. chili powder
- ½ tsp. ground cumin
- ¼ tsp. garlic powder

1. Preheat oven to 425°. Place potatoes in a greased 15x10x1-in. baking pan. Drizzle with oil; sprinkle with 1 tsp. salt and the pepper. Toss to coat. Roast until tender, 25-30 minutes, stirring occasionally.

2. In a large bowl, mix potatoes, beans, chiles and cilantro. In a small bowl, combine sour cream, mayonnaise, lime juice, chipotle pepper, cumin, garlic powder and remaining salt. Pour dressing over potato mixture; toss to coat. Serve warm.

|||||||||||||

¾ cup: 334 cal., 17g fat (4g sat. fat), 5mg chol., 588mg sod., 39g carb. (2g sugars, 6g fiber), 6g pro.

BEEFY
ENTREES

SUPER CALZONES

||||||||||||||||||||||||||||||||||

A friend gave this recipe to me at my wedding shower. I quickly realized that I'd better learn how to cook! My husband loves these handheld pizzas.
—Laronda Warrick, Parker, KS

PREP: 30 MIN.
BAKE: 20 MIN.
MAKES: 4 SERVINGS

- ½ lb. ground beef
- 2 Tbsp. finely chopped onion
- 2 Tbsp. finely chopped green pepper
- 1 garlic clove, minced
- 1 can (15 oz.) tomato sauce
- 1 tsp. Italian seasoning
- 1 tube (13.8 oz.) refrigerated pizza crust
- 3 oz. cream cheese, softened
- 1 cup shredded part-skim mozzarella cheese
- 1 can (4 oz.) mushroom stems and pieces, drained
- 1 can (2¼ oz.) sliced ripe olives, drained

1. In a large skillet, cook the beef, onion, green pepper and garlic over medium heat until meat is no longer pink; drain and set aside.

2. In a small saucepan, bring tomato sauce and Italian seasoning to a boil. Reduce heat; cover and simmer for 5 minutes. Stir ½ cup into the meat mixture; keep remaining sauce warm.

3. Unroll pizza crust onto a floured surface. Roll into a 12-in. square; cut into 4 squares. Spread cream cheese over each to within ½ in. of edges. Top with meat mixture. Sprinkle with mozzarella cheese, mushrooms and olives.

4. Fold dough over filling, forming a triangle; press edges with a fork to seal. Place on a greased baking sheet.

5. Bake at 400° for 20-25 minutes or until golden brown. Serve with the remaining sauce.

|||||||||||

1 calzone: 541 cal., 24g fat (11g sat. fat), 67mg chol., 1552mg sod., 58g carb. (10g sugars, 4g fiber), 28g pro.

SASSY SALSA
MEAT
LOAVES

IIIIIIIIIIIIIIIIIIIIIIIIIIIIIIIIII

*Here's a twist on classic meat
loaf that can be made ahead
and will last for a few days
afterward. Make meat loaf
sandwiches with the leftovers,
buns and slices of Monterey
Jack cheese.*
—Iasha Tully, Owings Mills, MD

PREP: 25 MIN.
BAKE: 65 MIN. + STANDING
MAKES: 2 LOAVES
(6 SERVINGS EACH)

- ¾ **cup uncooked instant brown rice**
- 1 **can (8 oz.) tomato sauce**
- 1½ **cups salsa, divided**
- 1 **large onion, chopped**
- 1 **large egg, lightly beaten**
- 1 **celery rib, finely chopped**
- ¼ **cup minced fresh parsley**
- 2 **Tbsp. minced fresh cilantro**
- 2 **garlic cloves, minced**
- 1 **Tbsp. chili powder**
- 1½ **tsp. salt**
- ½ **tsp. pepper**
- 2 **lbs. lean ground beef (90% lean)**
- 1 **lb. ground turkey**
- ½ **cup shredded reduced-fat Monterey Jack cheese or Mexican cheese blend**

1. Preheat oven to 350°. Cook rice according to package directions; cool slightly. In a large bowl, combine tomato sauce, ½ cup salsa, onion, egg, celery, parsley, cilantro, garlic and seasonings; stir in rice. Add the beef and turkey; mix lightly but thoroughly.

2. Shape into two 8x4-in. loaves in a greased 15x10x1-in. baking pan. Bake until a thermometer inserted in center reads 165°, 1-1¼ hours.

3. Spread with remaining salsa and sprinkle with cheese; bake until cheese is melted, about 5 minutes. Let stand 10 minutes before slicing.

FREEZE OPTION: Bake meat loaves without topping. Securely wrap and freeze cooled meat loaf in foil. To use, partially thaw in refrigerator overnight. Unwrap meat loaves; place in a greased 15x10x1-in. baking pan. Reheat in a preheated 350° oven until a thermometer inserted in center reads 165°, 40-45 minutes; top as directed.

IIIIIIIIIIIII

1 slice: 237 cal., 11g fat (4g sat. fat), 91mg chol., 634mg sod., 9g carb. (2g sugars, 1g fiber), 25g pro. Diabetic exchanges: 3 lean meat, ½ starch, ½ fat.

CUMIN-CHILI SPICED
FLANK STEAK

||||||||||||||||||||||||||||||||||

This is a wonderful meal-in-one dish to share with your family. They'll rave about the sizzling grilled flank steak served with a jalapeno and tomato salsa.

—Yvonne Starlin, Westmoreland, TN

PREP: 40 MIN.
COOK: 15 MIN.
MAKES: 4 SERVINGS

- 2 **small sweet red peppers, cut into 2-in. strips**
- 1 **small sweet yellow pepper, cut into 2-in. strips**
- 2 **cups grape tomatoes**
- 1 **small onion, cut into ½-in. wedges**
- 2 **jalapeno peppers, halved and seeded**
- 2 **Tbsp. olive oil, divided**
- ¾ **tsp. salt, divided**
- ¾ **tsp. pepper, divided**
- 2 **tsp. ground cumin**
- 1 **tsp. chili powder**
- 1 **beef flank steak (1½ lbs.)**
- 2 **to 3 tsp. lime juice**
  Hot cooked couscous
  Lime wedges

1. Preheat broiler. Place the first 5 ingredients in a greased 15x10x1-in. baking pan. Toss with 1 Tbsp. oil, ¼ tsp. salt and ¼ tsp. pepper. Broil 4 in. from heat 10-12 minutes or until vegetables are tender and begin to char, turning once.

2. Meanwhile, mix salt, pepper, cumin, chili powder and the remaining oil; rub over both sides of steak. Grill, covered, over medium heat or broil 4 in. from heat 6-9 minutes on each side or until meat reaches desired doneness (for medium-rare, a thermometer should read 135°; medium, 140°; medium-well, 145°). Let stand 5 minutes.

3. For salsa, chop broiled onion and jalapenos; place in a small bowl. Stir in tomatoes and lime juice. Thinly slice steak across the grain; serve with salsa, broiled peppers, couscous and lime wedges.

|||||||||||||

1 serving : 359 cal., 20g fat (6g sat. fat), 81mg chol., 562mg sod., 10g carb. (5g sugars, 3g fiber), 35g pro.

BEEF &
BLUE CHEESE TART

||||||||||||||||||||||||||||||||

This elegant, rustic recipe goes together in minutes and is so simple. It's just perfect for entertaining!
—Judy Batson, Tampa, FL

PREP: 20 MIN.
BAKE: 15 MIN.
MAKES: 6 SERVINGS

- ½ **lb. lean ground beef (90% lean)**
- 1¾ **cups sliced fresh mushrooms**
- ½ **medium red onion, thinly sliced**
- ¼ **tsp. salt**
- ¼ **tsp. pepper**
- 1 **tube (13.8 oz.) refrigerated pizza crust**
- ½ **cup reduced-fat sour cream**
- 2 **tsp. Italian seasoning**
- ½ **tsp. garlic powder**
- ¾ **cup crumbled blue cheese**

1. In a large skillet, cook the beef, mushrooms and onion over medium heat until meat is no longer pink; drain. Stir in salt and pepper; set aside.

2. On a lightly floured surface, roll crust into a 15x12-in. rectangle. Transfer to a parchment-lined baking sheet.

3. In a small bowl, combine the sour cream, Italian seasoning and garlic powder; spread over crust to within 2 in. of edges. Spoon beef mixture over top. Fold up edges of crust over filling, leaving center uncovered.

4. Bake at 425° for 15-18 minutes or until crust is golden. Using the parchment, slide tart onto a wire rack. Sprinkle with blue cheese; let stand for 5 minutes before slicing.

|||||||||||||

1 slice: 328 cal., 12g fat (5g sat. fat), 43mg chol., 803mg sod., 35g carb. (6g sugars, 1g fiber), 19g pro. Diabetic exchanges: 2 starch, 2 lean meat, 2 fat.

EASY STUFFED
POBLANOS

IIIIIIIIIIIIIIIIIIIIIIIIIIIIIIIIIIII

*My partner adores these saucy
stuffed peppers—and I love
how quickly the dish comes
together. Top with low-fat sour
cream and your favorite salsa.*
—Jean Erhardt, Portland, OR

TAKES: 25 MIN.
MAKES: 4 SERVINGS

- ½ **lb. Italian turkey
  sausage links, casings
  removed**
- ½ **lb. lean ground beef
  (90% lean)**
- 1 **pkg. (8.8 oz.) ready-to-
  serve Spanish rice**
- 4 **large poblano peppers**
- 1 **cup enchilada sauce**
- ½ **cup shredded Mexican
  cheese blend
  Minced fresh cilantro,
  optional**

1. Preheat broiler. In a large skillet, cook turkey and beef over medium heat until no longer pink, 5-7 minutes, breaking into crumbles; drain.

2. Prepare rice according to package directions. Add rice to meat mixture.

3. Cut peppers lengthwise in half; remove seeds. Place on a foil-lined 15x10x1-in. baking pan, cut side down. Broil 4 in. from heat until skins blister, about 5 minutes. With tongs, turn peppers.

4. Fill with turkey mixture; top with enchilada sauce and sprinkle with cheese. Broil until cheese is melted, 1-2 minutes longer. If desired, top with cilantro.

IIIIIIIIIIII

*2 stuffed pepper halves: 312 cal., 13g fat (4g sat. fat),
63mg chol., 1039mg sod., 27g carb. (5g sugars, 2g fiber),
22g pro.*

> **Planned Overs:** *If you have leftover rice you'd like to use up, simply swap out the Spanish rice called for here. You'll need about 2 cups cooked rice for the filling.*

GROUND BEEF
WELLINGTONS

IIIIIIIIIIIIIIIIIIIIIIIIIIIIIIIIII

*Trying new recipes is one of my
favorite hobbies. It's also the
most gratifying. This recipe is
easy enough for weeknights
yet it's impressive enough for
holidays and special occasions.*
—Julie Frankamp, Nicollet, MN

PREP: 30 MIN.
BAKE: 25 MIN.
MAKES: 2 SERVINGS

- ½ cup chopped fresh mushrooms
- 1 Tbsp. butter
- 2 tsp. all-purpose flour
- ¼ tsp. pepper, divided
- ½ cup half-and-half cream
- 1 large egg yolk
- 2 Tbsp. finely chopped onion
- ¼ tsp. salt
- ½ lb. ground beef
- 1 tube (4 oz.) refrigerated crescent rolls
  Large egg, lightly beaten, optional
- 1 tsp. dried parsley flakes

1. In a saucepan, saute mushrooms in butter until softened. Stir in flour and ⅛ tsp. pepper until blended. Gradually add the cream. Bring to a boil; cook and stir until thickened, about 2 minutes. Remove from the heat and set aside.

2. In a bowl, combine the egg yolk, onion, 2 Tbsp. mushroom sauce, salt and remaining ⅛ tsp. pepper. Crumble beef over mixture and mix well. Shape into 2 loaves. Separate crescent dough into 2 rectangles on a baking sheet. Seal perforations. Place a meat loaf on each rectangle. Bring dough edges together and pinch to seal. If desired, brush with egg wash. Bake at 350° until golden brown and a thermometer inserted into meat loaf reads 160°, 24-28 minutes.

3. Meanwhile, warm remaining sauce over low heat; stir in parsley. Serve sauce with Wellingtons.

IIIIIIIIIIIII

1 serving: 570 cal., 37g fat (16g sat. fat), 207mg chol., 909mg sod., 28g carb. (7g sugars, 1g fiber), 28g pro.

READER REVIEW
"This is absolutely heavenly and easy. I made it with mashed potatoes. I may double the sauce next time as it was so good!"
—MABALL, TASTEOFHOME.COM

CORNISH PASTIES

||||||||||||||||||||||||||||||||

My great-aunt Gladys was from a small mining town in England where pasties were popular. I loved to watch her craft each Cornish pasty, as she would make them in different sizes depending on who was eating. Serve these with a green salad to make a wonderful meal.
—Verna Hainer, Pueblo, CO

PREP: 30 MIN. + CHILLING
BAKE: 50 MIN.
MAKES: 8 SERVINGS

3	cups all-purpose flour
1½	tsp. salt
¾	tsp. baking powder
1	cup shortening
8	to 10 Tbsp. ice water

FILLING

1	lb. beef top round steak, cut into ½-in. pieces
1½	cups finely chopped onion
1½	cups cubed peeled potatoes (½-in. cubes)
1½	cups chopped peeled turnips (½-in. cubes)
1	tsp. salt
¼	tsp. pepper
4	Tbsp. butter
½	cup evaporated milk, optional Ketchup

1. In a large bowl, mix flour, salt and baking powder; cut in shortening until crumbly. Gradually add water, tossing with a fork until dough forms a ball. Cover and refrigerate for 30 minutes.

2. Preheat oven to 375°. In another large bowl, combine beef, onion, potatoes, turnips, salt and pepper. Divide dough into 4 equal portions. On a lightly floured surface, roll 1 portion into a 9-in. circle. Mound 1½ cups filling on half of circle; dot with 1 Tbsp. butter. Moisten edges with water; fold dough over filling and press edges with a fork to seal.

3. Place on a parchment-lined rimmed 15x10x1-in. baking pan. Repeat with the remaining dough, filling and butter. Cut slits in tops of pasties. Bake 30 minutes. If desired, pour evaporated milk into slits. Bake until golden brown, 20-30 minutes longer. Serve with ketchup.

FREEZE OPTION: Freeze cooled pasties in a freezer container. To use, reheat pasties on a parchment-lined baking sheet in a preheated 375° oven until heated through.

||||||||||||

½ pasty: 556 cal., 32g fat (10g sat. fat), 47mg chol., 864mg sod., 46g carb. (3g sugars, 3g fiber), 19g pro.

CHEESEBURGER
BISCUITS

IIIIIIIIIIIIIIIIIIIIIIIIIIIIIIIIII

*Ground beef is my favorite
meat to cook with because
it's versatile and economical.
There's always a fun new
recipe to try, like these cheesy
burger biscuits.*
—Pat Chambless, Crowder, OK

PREP: 30 MIN.
BAKE: 10 MIN.
MAKES: 5 SERVINGS

- ½ **lb. ground beef**
- 1 **Tbsp. chopped onion**
- ½ **tsp. salt**
- ⅛ **tsp. pepper**
- 1 **tube (12 oz.) refrigerated buttermilk biscuits**
- 5 **slices process American cheese**

1. Preheat oven to 400°. In a large skillet, cook beef, onion, salt and pepper over medium heat until meat is no longer pink; drain and cool.

2. Place 2 biscuits overlapping on a floured surface; roll out into a 5-in. oval. Place about ¼ cup of meat mixture on 1 side. Fold a cheese slice to fit over meat mixture. Fold dough over filling; press edges with a fork to seal. Repeat with remaining biscuits, meat mixture and cheese.

3. Place on a greased baking sheet. Prick tops with a fork. Bake 10 minutes or until golden brown.

IIIIIIIIIIIII

1 serving: 299 cal., 10g fat (5g sat. fat), 36mg chol., 1101mg sod., 34g carb. (1g sugars, 0 fiber), 17g pro.

Expert Secret: Pricking the tops of cheeseburger pockets helps steam escape during baking. If you don't do this, the pockets will puff up and may break open.

DAD'S FAVORITE
BARBECUE MEAT LOAVES

||||||||||||||||||||||||||||||||||||

It may sound old-fashioned, but it warms my heart to serve dishes that make my family and friends happy. This recipe does just that, and then some.
—Leta Winters, Johnson City, TN

TAKES: 30 MIN.
MAKES: 4 SERVINGS

1	**large egg, lightly beaten**
½	**cup stuffing mix, crushed**
3	**Tbsp. 2% milk**
2	**Tbsp. grated Parmesan cheese**
1	**Tbsp. plus ¼ cup barbecue sauce, divided**
1	**lb. ground beef**

1. Preheat oven to 425°. In a large bowl, combine egg, stuffing mix, milk, cheese and 1 Tbsp. barbecue sauce. Add beef; mix lightly but thoroughly. Shape into four 4x2-in. loaves in a foil-lined 15x10x1-in. baking pan.

2. Bake until a thermometer reads 160°, 15-20 minutes. Spread with remaining barbecue sauce before serving.

FREEZE OPTION: Individually wrap cooled meat loaves in plastic and foil, then freeze. To use, partially thaw the meat loaves in refrigerator overnight. Unwrap loaves; reheat in a greased 15x10x1-in. baking pan in a preheated 350° oven until loaves are heated through and a thermometer inserted in center reads 165°. Top each with 1 Tbsp. barbecue sauce before serving.

|||||||||||||

1 mini meat loaf: 305 cal., 16g fat (6g sat. fat), 120mg chol., 449mg sod., 15g carb. (8g sugars, 1g fiber), 24g pro.

MEATBALL
FLATBREAD

IIIIIIIIIIIIIIIIIIIIIIIIIIIIIIII

*As amazing as this flatbread
tastes, you would never know
how quickly it comes together.
A little hidden carrot, unnoticed
by the kids, adds sweet texture.
For a crispier crust, bake the
flatbread in the oven until it is
slightly crispy on top before
applying the tomato sauce.*
—Kimberly Berg, North Street, MI

TAKES: 25 MIN.
MAKES: 4 FLATBREADS

  1   **can (15 oz.) Italian
      tomato sauce**
  1   **medium carrot, coarsely
      chopped**
  3   **fresh basil leaves**
  1   **garlic clove, halved**
  4   **naan flatbreads**
  2   **cups shredded
      mozzarella cheese**
 14   **frozen fully cooked
      Italian meatballs,
      thawed and halved
      Dash each salt, pepper,
      dried parsley flakes and
      dried oregano**

1. Preheat oven to 400°. Place tomato sauce, carrot, basil and
garlic in a food processor; cover and process until pureed.

2. Place flatbreads on an ungreased baking sheet. Spread with
tomato sauce mixture; top with cheese and meatballs. Sprinkle
with seasonings.

3. Bake on a lower oven rack until cheese melts, 12-15 minutes.

IIIIIIIIIIIII

*½ flatbread: 228 cal., 10g fat (5g sat. fat), 46mg chol.,
835mg sod., 21g carb. (3g sugars, 2g fiber), 14g pro.*

HOBO DINNER

||||||||||||||||||||||||||||||||||||||||

The meat and vegetables in this effortless dinner are all wrapped in a piece of foil and cooked together on a baking sheet. The recipe yields a single serving, but you could easily make as many meal-in-one packets as you need.
—Pat Walter, Pine Island, MN

PREP: 5 MIN.
BAKE: 45 MIN.
MAKES: 1 SERVING

¼   **lb. ground beef**
1   **potato, sliced**
1   **carrot, sliced**
2   **Tbsp. chopped onion**
1   **sheet heavy-duty aluminum foil (18 in. x 13 in.)**
    Salt and pepper to taste, optional

Shape beef into a patty; place in the center of foil with potato, carrot and onion. Sprinkle with salt and pepper if desired. Fold foil over and seal well; place on a baking sheet. Bake at 350° for 45 minutes. Open foil carefully.

|||||||||||||||

1 serving: 374 cal., 9g fat (4g sat. fat), 69mg chol., 84mg sod., 46g carb. (8g sugars, 6g fiber), 27g pro.

MEAT LOAF
CORDON BLEU

||||||||||||||||||||||||||||||||

I'm a school counselor and mother of a young child. Even with my busy schedule, I can make this in the morning, set it in the fridge, and pop it into the oven when I get home.
—Barb Jacobsen, Campbell, NE

PREP: 15 MIN.
BAKE: 1¼ HOURS
MAKES: 10 SERVINGS

1 large egg, beaten
1 envelope meat loaf seasoning mix
⅓ cup tomato sauce
2 cups soft bread crumbs
2 lbs. lean ground beef
8 thin slices fully cooked ham
8 thin slices Swiss cheese
1 can (4 oz.) sliced mushrooms

In a large bowl, mix together egg, meat loaf seasoning, tomato sauce and bread crumbs. Add ground beef; mix well. On a piece of waxed paper, pat meat mixture into an 18x9-in. rectangle. Top with layers of ham, cheese and mushrooms. Roll rectangle, jelly-roll style, starting from narrow end. Pinch edges to seal. Place seam side down in a shallow baking pan. Bake at 350° until no pink remains, about 1¼ hours. Let stand several minutes before slicing.

FREEZE OPTION: Securely wrap and freeze cooled meat loaf in foil. To use, partially thaw in refrigerator overnight. Unwrap meat loaf; reheat on a greased 15x10x1-in. baking pan in a preheated 350° oven until heated through and a thermometer inserted in center reads 165°.

||||||||||||

1 slice. 287 cal., 14g fat (7g sat fat), 105mg chol., 659mg sod., 10g carb. (1g sugars, 1g fiber), 28g pro.

MOZZARELLA
BEEF
ROLL-UPS

|||||||||||||||||||||||||||||||||

The kids will love these pepperoni and beef wraps. They're easy to assemble because each tortilla is simply wrapped around a portion of hearty meat filling with a piece of string cheese.
—*Taste of Home* Test Kitchen

TAKES: 30 MIN.
MAKES: 6 SERVINGS

1 **lb. ground beef**
1 **medium green pepper, chopped**
⅓ **cup chopped onion**
1 **can (8 oz.) pizza sauce**
2 **oz. sliced pepperoni (about ⅔ cup)**
½ **tsp. dried oregano**
6 **flour tortillas (10 in.), warmed**
6 **pieces string cheese (about 6 oz.)**

1. Preheat oven to 350°. In a large skillet, cook and crumble beef with pepper and onion over medium-high heat until no longer pink, 5-7 minutes; drain. Stir in pizza sauce, pepperoni and oregano.

2. Spoon ½ cup mixture across center of each tortilla; top with a piece of string cheese. Fold bottom and sides of tortilla over filling and roll up.

3. Place on an ungreased baking sheet, seam side down. Bake until heated through, about 10 minutes.

FREEZE OPTION: Cool beef mixture before assembly. Individually wrap roll-ups in foil and freeze in a freezer container. To use, partially thaw overnight in refrigerator. Reheat foil-wrapped roll-ups on a baking sheet in a preheated 350° oven until heated through. To reheat individually, remove foil and rewrap in paper towel; place on a microwave-safe plate. Microwave on high until heated through, turning once. Let stand 15 seconds.

|||||||||||||

1 roll-up: 513 cal., 25g fat (11g sat. fat), 71mg chol., 1064mg sod., 41g carb. (5g sugars, 4g fiber), 30g pro.

EASY
BEEF PIES

||||||||||||||||||||||||||||||||||||

We make a lot of French dips and always have leftover roast beef—I put it to good use in these pies.
—Jennie Weber, Palmer, AK

TAKES: 30 MIN.
MAKES: 4 SERVINGS

- 1 pkg. (15 oz.) refrigerated beef roast au jus
- 1 Tbsp. canola oil
- ¼ cup finely chopped onion
- ¼ cup finely chopped green pepper
- 1 garlic clove, minced
- 2 sheets refrigerated pie crust
- 1 cup shredded Mexican cheese blend
  Salsa con queso dip, optional

1. Preheat oven to 425°. Drain beef, reserving ¼ cup juices; shred meat with 2 forks. In a large skillet, heat canola oil over medium-high heat. Add onion and pepper; cook and stir until tender, 1-2 minutes. Add minced garlic; cook 30 seconds longer. Remove from heat; stir in beef and reserved juices.

2. Unroll 1 pie crust; cut in half. Layer ¼ cup shredded cheese and about ⅓ cup beef mixture over each crust half to within ½ in. of edge. Fold crusts over filling; press edges with a fork to seal. Place on a greased baking sheet. Repeat with the remaining crust and filling.

3. Bake until golden brown, 15-18 minutes. If desired, serve with queso dip.

FREEZE OPTION: Freeze cooled pies in a freezer container. To use, reheat pies on a greased baking sheet in a preheated 350° oven until heated through.

||||||||||||

1 pie: 752 cal., 46g fat (19g sat. fat), 108mg chol., 921mg sod., 53g carb. (7g sugars, 0 fiber), 31g pro.

STAR OF THE NORTH
PASTIES

IIIIIIIIIIIIIIIIIIIIIIIIIIIIIIIIIIII

As a twist on a traditional English meat pie, these pasties will delight your family. They are so quick to assemble and disappear just as fast.
—Bonnie Gelle, Grand Rapids, MN

PREP: 30 MIN.
BAKE: 1 HOUR
MAKES: 4 SERVINGS

- 2   cups all-purpose flour
- ½   tsp. salt
- ½   tsp. baking powder
- ½   cup shortening or lard
- ½   cup 2% milk
- ½   cup cubed uncooked potatoes
- ½   cup cubed uncooked rutabagas
- ½   cup cubed uncooked carrots
- ¼   cup chopped onion
- ½   lb. ground beef or diced beef top sirloin steak, browned

1. Mix together first 3 ingredients; cut in shortening to form particles the size of large peas. Gradually add milk and mix just enough to make mixture stick together. Lightly shape dough into 4 balls; let stand for 5 minutes.

2. Meanwhile, combine vegetables and meat. On a lightly floured surface, roll each ball into a circle. Place one-fourth of the vegetable/meat mixture on 1 side of each circle; brush edge of crust with water and fold half the dough over filling. Press edges together to seal. Place on an ungreased baking sheet and prick tops with a fork. Bake at 350° for 1 hour.

IIIIIIIIIIIII

1 pasty: 588 cal., 31g fat (9g sat. fat), 32mg chol., 409mg sod., 57g carb. (5g sugars, 3g fiber), 18g pro.

READER REVIEW
"I grew up in northern Minnesota, and these pasties are just like I remember! They are great in cold-weather months. I do like to add a bit of dried parsley and thyme."
—SUGARCRYSTAL, TASTEOFHOME.COM

SHEET-PAN
TACO SALAD

|||||||||||||||||||||||||||||||||

*This tasty taco salad is packed
with beef, cheese, tomato and
enough satisfying Southwest
flavor to make everyone happy.*
—Jolene Young, Union, IL

PREP: 45 MIN.
BAKE: 25 MIN.
MAKES: 10 SERVINGS

2½ **lbs. lean ground beef
(90% lean)**
1 **envelope taco seasoning**
1 **can (8 oz.) tomato sauce**
¾ **cup water**
1 **pkg. (15½ oz.) nacho-
flavored tortilla chips,
crushed**
2 **cups shredded Monterey
Jack cheese**
2 **cups shredded cheddar
cheese**
4 **cups torn iceberg lettuce**
1 **medium red onion, finely
chopped**
10 **slices tomato, halved**
1 **cup sour cream**
10 **pitted ripe olives, halved**

1. Preheat oven to 325°. In a 6-qt. stockpot, cook and crumble beef over medium-high heat until no longer pink, 7-9 minutes. Stir in seasoning, tomato sauce and water; bring to a boil. Reduce heat; simmer, uncovered, 15 minutes, stirring occasionally.

2. Spread chips evenly in a greased 15x10x1-in. baking pan; sprinkle with Monterey Jack cheese. Top with the ground beef mixture; sprinkle with cheddar cheese. Bake until bubbly, 25-30 minutes.

3. Cut into ten 5x3-in. portions. Top each serving with lettuce, onion, tomatoes, sour cream and olives.

|||||||||||||

*1 serving: 569 cal., 35g fat (13g sat. fat), 99mg chol.,
962mg sod., 35g carb. (4g sugars, 3g fiber), 32g pro.*

BROCCOLI
BEEF
BRAIDS

||||||||||||||||||||||||||||||||

*Each slice of this delicious
golden bread is like a hot
sandwich packed with beef,
broccoli and mozzarella.*
—Penny Lapp, North Royalton, OH

TAKES: 30 MIN.
MAKES: 2 LOAVES
(4 SERVINGS EACH)

1   **lb. ground beef**
½   **cup chopped onion**
3   **cups frozen chopped
     broccoli**
1   **cup shredded part-skim
     mozzarella cheese**
½   **cup sour cream**
¼   **tsp. salt**
¼   **tsp. pepper**
2   **tubes (8 oz. each)
     refrigerated crescent
     rolls**

1. Preheat oven to 350°. In a large skillet, cook beef and onion over medium heat 6-8 minutes or until beef is no longer pink, breaking up beef into crumbles; drain. Stir in broccoli, cheese, sour cream, salt and pepper; heat through.

2. Unroll 1 tube of crescent dough onto a greased baking sheet; form into a 12x8-in. rectangle, pressing perforations to seal. Spoon half of the beef mixture lengthwise down center of rectangle.

3. On each long side, cut 1-in.-wide strips at an angle, about 3 in. into the center. Fold 1 strip from each side over filling and pinch ends together; repeat.

4. Repeat with remaining ingredients to make second braid. Bake 15-20 minutes or until golden brown.

|||||||||||||

1 piece: 396 cal., 23g fat (6g sat. fat), 48mg chol., 644mg sod., 29g carb. (8g sugars, 2g fiber), 20g pro.

MINI MEDITERRANEAN
PIZZA

|||||||||||||||||||||||||||||||||||||||

I was on a mini pizza kick and had already served up Mexican and Italian variations, so I opted for a Mediterranean version and came up with these.

— Jenny Dubinsky, Inwood, WV

PREP: 30 MIN.
BAKE: 5 MIN.
MAKES: 4 SERVINGS

1	Tbsp. olive oil
8	oz. lean ground beef (90% lean)
¼	cup finely chopped onion
2	garlic cloves, minced
1	can (8 oz.) tomato sauce
1	tsp. minced fresh rosemary or ¼ tsp. dried rosemary, crushed
2	whole wheat pita breads (6 in.), cut in half horizontally
1	medium tomato, seeded and chopped
½	cup fresh baby spinach, thinly sliced
12	Greek pitted olives, thinly sliced
½	cup shredded part-skim mozzarella cheese
¼	cup crumbled feta cheese

1. Heat oil in a large nonstick skillet; cook the beef, onion and garlic over medium heat until meat is no longer pink, 5-6 minutes; drain. Stir in tomato sauce and rosemary; bring to a boil. Reduce heat; simmer, uncovered, until thickened, 6-9 minutes.

2. Place pita halves, cut side up, on a baking sheet. Top with meat mixture, tomato, spinach and olives. Sprinkle with cheeses. Bake at 400° until cheeses are melted, 4-6 minutes.

|||||||||||||

1 pizza: 287 cal., 12g fat (5g sat. fat), 47mg chol., 783mg sod., 25g carb. (3g sugars, 4g fiber), 21g pro. Diabetic exchanges: 2 lean meat, 1½ starch, 1 fat.

POULTRY
DINNERS
||||||||||||||||||||||

SHORTCUT
CHICKEN CHIMICHANGAS

||||||||||||||||||||||||||||||||

Mimic the crunch of a fried chimichanga by brushing these with oil and baking them. Our children love to have them when they get home late after school activities.
—Johnna Johnson, Scottsdale, AZ

PREP: 35 MIN.
BAKE: 15 MIN.
MAKES: 6 SERVINGS

- ¼ **cup canola oil, divided**
- 1 **small onion, chopped**
- 1 **rotisserie chicken, skin removed, shredded (about 3½ cups)**
- 1 **pkg. (8.8 oz.) ready-to-serve long grain rice**
- 1 **can (15 oz.) black beans, rinsed and drained**
- 1 **can (4 oz.) chopped green chiles**
- 2 **tsp. minced chipotle peppers in adobo sauce**
- ¼ **tsp. ground cumin**
- ¼ **tsp. salt**
- ¼ **tsp. pepper**
- 1½ **cups shredded Mexican cheese blend**
- ⅓ **cup chopped fresh cilantro**
- 6 **flour tortillas (10 in.), warmed**
  Salsa

1. Preheat oven to 425°. Place a 15x10x1-in. baking pan in the oven.

2. In a large skillet, heat 2 Tbsp. oil over medium-high heat; saute onion until lightly browned, about 5 minutes. Stir in chicken, rice, beans, chiles, chipotle peppers, cumin, salt and pepper; cook until heated through. Remove from heat; stir in cheese and cilantro.

3. Spoon 1 cup chicken mixture across bottom third of each tortilla. Fold bottom and sides of tortilla over filling and roll up. Brush preheated baking pan with some of the remaining oil. Place chimichangas seam side down; brush tortillas with oil. Bake until crisp and golden, about 15 minutes, turning halfway through baking. Serve with salsa.

||||||||||||

1 chimichanga: 704 cal., 31g fat (9g sat. fat), 98mg chol., 1081mg sod., 62g carb. (4g sugars, 6g fiber), 41g pro.

Quick Fix: *Use 2 cups leftover cooked rice in place of the package of ready-to-serve rice.*

HOISIN SRIRACHA
SHEET-PAN CHICKEN

||||||||||||||||||||||||||||||||

The convenience and simplicity of this chicken dinner make it extra awesome. Feel free to change the veggies throughout the year, because the sticky-spicy-sweet sauce is tasty on everything!
—Julie Peterson, Crofton, MD

PREP: 20 MIN.
BAKE: 40 MIN.
MAKES: 4 SERVINGS

- ⅓ cup hoisin sauce
- ⅓ cup reduced-sodium soy sauce
- 2 Tbsp. maple syrup
- 2 Tbsp. Sriracha chili sauce
- 1 Tbsp. rice vinegar
- 2 tsp. sesame oil
- 2 garlic cloves, minced
- ½ tsp. minced fresh gingerroot
- 4 bone-in chicken thighs (6 oz. each)
- ¼ tsp. salt
- ¼ tsp. pepper
- 1 medium sweet potato, cut into ¾-in. cubes
- 2 Tbsp. olive oil, divided
- 4 cups fresh cauliflowerets
- 1 medium sweet red pepper, cut into ¾-in. pieces
  Sesame seeds, optional

1. Preheat oven to 400°. Whisk together the first 8 ingredients. Set aside.

2. Sprinkle both sides of chicken with salt and pepper. Place the chicken and sweet potato in a single layer in a foil-lined 15x10x1-in. baking pan. Drizzle with 1 Tbsp. olive oil and a third of the hoisin mixture; toss to coat.

3. Bake 15 minutes; turn chicken and potatoes. Add cauliflower and red pepper; drizzle with another third of the hoisin mixture and the remaining olive oil. Bake until a thermometer inserted in chicken reads 170°-175°, about 25 minutes longer. Drizzle with the remaining hoisin mixture. If desired, sprinkle with sesame seeds.

|||||||||||||

1 serving: 490 cal., 24g fat (5g sat. fat), 81mg chol., 1665mg sod., 40g carb. (23g sugars, 5g fiber), 28g pro.

Have It Your Way: *Broccoli is an easy substitute for the cauliflower in this flavorful dish.*

ITALIAN CHEESE
TURKEY
BURGERS

IIIIIIIIIIIIIIIIIIIIIIIIIIIIIIII

*My husband is picky about his
burgers, and he loves these!
We eat burgers a lot in warm
weather, so I cut down on fat
and calories by spicing up
ground turkey.*
—Brenda DiMarco, Whiteford, MD

PREP: 15 MIN.
BAKE: 20 MIN.
MAKES: 6 SERVINGS

- ½ cup sun-dried tomatoes (not packed in oil)
- ¾ cup boiling water
- 1 large egg white, beaten
- ½ cup dry bread crumbs
- 1 small onion, finely chopped
- ¼ cup ketchup
- 1 Tbsp. minced fresh basil or 1 tsp. dried basil
- 1 Tbsp. minced fresh parsley
- 1 Tbsp. spicy brown mustard
- 2 garlic cloves, minced
- 1 tsp. dried oregano
- ¼ tsp. Italian seasoning
- 1 lb. lean ground turkey
- ½ lb. extra-lean ground turkey
- 3 slices reduced-fat provolone cheese, halved
- 6 whole wheat hamburger buns, split
  Optional: Ketchup and mustard

1. Place tomatoes in a small bowl; add boiling water. Cover and let stand for 5 minutes.

2. In a large bowl, combine the egg white, bread crumbs, onion, ketchup, basil, parsley, mustard, garlic, oregano and Italian seasoning. Drain and chop tomatoes; add to egg white mixture. Crumble the turkey over mixture and mix well. Shape into 6 burgers.

3. Place in a 15x10x1-in. baking pan coated with cooking spray. Bake at 350° for 16-20 minutes or until a thermometer reads 165° and juices run clear. Top with cheese; bake 1-2 minutes longer or until melted. Serve on buns. Top with ketchup and mustard as desired.

IIIIIIIIIIIII

*1 burger: 362 cal., 11g fat (3g sat. fat), 80mg chol.,
698mg sod., 35g carb. (9g sugars, 5g fiber), 31g pro.
Diabetic exchanges: 4 lean meat, 2 starch.*

CHICKEN
VEGGIE
PACKETS

IIIIIIIIIIIIIIIIIIIIIIIIIIIIIIIIIIIIIIIII

People think I went to a lot of trouble when I serve these packets. Individual aluminum foil pouches hold in the juices during baking to keep the herbed chicken moist and tender. It saves time and makes cleanup a breeze.
—Edna Shaffer, Beulah, MI

TAKES: 30 MIN.
MAKES: 4 SERVINGS

4	**boneless skinless chicken breast halves** (4 oz. each)
½	**lb. sliced fresh mushrooms**
1½	**cups fresh baby carrots**
1	**cup pearl onions**
½	**cup julienned sweet red pepper**
¼	**tsp. pepper**
3	**tsp. minced fresh thyme**
½	**tsp. salt, optional** Lemon wedges, optional

1. Flatten the chicken breasts to ½-in. thickness; place each on a piece of heavy-duty foil (about 12 in. square). Layer the mushrooms, carrots, onions and red pepper over chicken; sprinkle with pepper, thyme and, if desired, salt.

2. Fold foil around chicken and vegetables and seal tightly. Place on a baking sheet. Bake at 375° for 20 minutes or until chicken juices run clear. If desired, serve with lemon wedges.

IIIIIIIIIIIIII

1 serving: 175 cal., 3g fat (1g sat. fat), 63mg chol., 100mg sod., 11g carb. (6g sugars, 2g fiber), 25g pro. Diabetic exchanges: 3 lean meat, 2 vegetable.

BUFFALO CHICKEN STUFFED
POBLANO PEPPERS

IIIIIIIIIIIIIIIIIIIIIIIIIIIIIIII

Since I do not like green bell peppers, I decided to create a filling that would go well with my favorite pepper, the poblano. After a few taste tests, my family deemed this entree a thumbs-up winner! I have also added black beans, used Cubanelle peppers and served cilantro lime rice on the side.
—Lorri Stout, Gaithersburg, MD

PREP: 15 MIN.
BAKE: 30 MIN.
MAKES: 8 SERVINGS

- 4   poblano peppers
- 2   Tbsp. butter
- 4   green onions, thinly sliced, divided
- 3   cups shredded cooked chicken breast
- 1   cup frozen corn (about 5 oz.), thawed
- 4   oz. cream cheese, cubed
- ¾   cup shredded Mexican cheese blend, divided
- ½   cup Buffalo wing sauce
- ¼   cup crumbled blue cheese
- 1   tsp. granulated garlic

1. Preheat oven to 350°. Cut peppers lengthwise in half; remove the seeds. Place in a greased 15x10x1-in. baking pan. In a large skillet, heat butter over medium-high heat. Add 3 green onions, sliced; cook and stir until tender, about 5 minutes. Add chicken, corn, cream cheese, ½ cup shredded cheese, wing sauce, blue cheese and garlic; cook and stir until cheeses are melted.

2. Fill the pepper halves with chicken mixture. Bake, covered, 25-30 minutes. Sprinkle with the remaining ¼ cup shredded cheese and sliced green onion; bake, uncovered, until the cheese is melted, about 5 minutes.

IIIIIIIIIIIIII

1 stuffed pepper half: 246 cal., 14g fat (8g sat. fat), 75mg chol., 668mg sod., 9g carb. (3g sugars, 2g fiber), 21g pro.

READER REVIEW
"Love this recipe! Heat level was perfect. Filling was creamy. We served ours with ranch dressing on the side."
—JSTOWELLSUPERMOM, TASTEOFHOME.COM

GINGER-CASHEW
CHICKEN SALAD

IIIIIIIIIIIIIIIIIIIIIIIIIIIIIIIIII

I revamped an Asian-style chicken salad recipe to create this gingery, crunchy salad. Now it's a huge success when I serve it at ladies luncheons.
—Shelly Gramer, Long Beach, CA

PREP: 20 MIN. + MARINATING
BROIL: 10 MIN.
MAKES: 8 SERVINGS

- ½ cup cider vinegar
- ½ cup molasses
- ⅓ cup canola oil
- 2 Tbsp. minced fresh gingerroot
- 2 tsp. reduced-sodium soy sauce
- 1 tsp. salt
- ⅛ tsp. cayenne pepper
- 4 boneless skinless chicken breast halves (6 oz. each)

SALAD
- 8 oz. fresh baby spinach (about 10 cups)
- 1 can (11 oz.) mandarin oranges, drained
- 1 cup shredded red cabbage
- 2 medium carrots, shredded
- 3 green onions, thinly sliced
- 2 cups chow mein noodles
- ¾ cup salted cashews, toasted
- 2 Tbsp. sesame seeds, toasted

1. In a small bowl, whisk the first 7 ingredients until blended. Pour ¾ cup marinade into a large shallow dish. Add chicken; turn to coat. Cover and refrigerate at least 3 hours. Cover and refrigerate remaining marinade.

2. Preheat broiler. Drain chicken, discarding marinade in dish. Place chicken in a 15x10x1-in. baking pan. Broil 4-6 in. from heat 4-6 minutes on each side or until a thermometer reads 165°. Cut chicken into strips.

3. Place spinach on a serving platter. Arrange chicken, oranges, cabbage, carrots and green onions on top. Sprinkle with chow mein noodles, cashews and sesame seeds. Stir the reserved molasses mixture; drizzle over salad and toss to coat. Serve immediately.

IIIIIIIIIIII

1½ cups: 379 cal., 18g fat (3g sat. fat), 47mg chol., 533mg sod., 33g carb. (16g sugars, 3g fiber), 23g pro. Diabetic exchanges: 2½ fat, 2 lean meat, 1½ starch, 1 vegetable.

SNEAKY TURKEY
MEATBALLS

||||||||||||||||||||||||||||||||||

Like most kids, mine refuse to eat certain veggies. In order to get healthy foods into their diets, I have to be sneaky. This recipe's vegetables give the meatballs a pleasing texture while providing a few nutrients. And I'm happy to say that my kids love 'em.

—Courtney Stultz, Weir, KS

PREP: 15 MIN.
BAKE: 20 MIN.
MAKES: 6 SERVINGS

- ¼ head cauliflower, broken into florets
- ½ cup finely shredded cabbage
- 1 Tbsp. potato starch or cornstarch
- 1 Tbsp. balsamic vinegar
- 1 tsp. sea salt
- 1 tsp. dried basil
- ½ tsp. pepper
- 1 lb. ground turkey
  Optional: Barbecue sauce and fresh basil leaves

1. Preheat oven to 400°. Place cauliflower in a food processor; pulse until finely chopped. Transfer to a large bowl. Add the cabbage, potato starch, vinegar, salt, basil and pepper.

2. Add turkey; mix lightly but thoroughly. With an ice cream scoop or with wet hands, shape into 1½-in. balls. Place the meatballs on a greased rack in a 15x10x1-in. baking pan. Bake 20-24 minutes or until cooked through. If desired, toss with barbecue sauce and top with basil.

||||||||||||||

2 meatballs: 125 cal., 6g fat (1g sat. fat), 50mg chol., 370mg sod., 4g carb. (1g sugars, 1g fiber), 15g pro. Diabetic exchanges: 2 medium-fat meat.

SHEET-PAN
CHICKEN PARMESAN

||||||||||||||||||||||||||||||||||

Saucy chicken, melty mozzarella and crisp-tender broccoli—all in one pan. What could be better?
— Becky Hardin, St. Peters, MO

PREP: 15 MIN.
BAKE: 25 MIN.
MAKES: 4 SERVINGS

- 1 **large egg**
- ½ **cup panko bread crumbs**
- ½ **cup grated Parmesan cheese**
- ½ **tsp. salt**
- 1 **tsp. pepper**
- 1 **tsp. garlic powder**
- 4 **boneless skinless chicken breast halves (6 oz. each)**
  Olive oil-flavored cooking spray
- 4 **cups fresh or frozen broccoli florets (about 10 oz.)**
- 1 **cup marinara sauce**
- 1 **cup shredded mozzarella cheese**
- ¼ **cup minced fresh basil, optional**

1. Preheat oven to 400°. Lightly coat a 15x10x1-in. baking pan with cooking spray.

2. In a shallow bowl, whisk egg. In a separate shallow bowl, stir together the next 5 ingredients. Dip chicken breast in egg; allow excess to drip off. Then dip in crumb mixture, patting to help coating adhere. Repeat with remaining chicken. Place chicken breasts in center third of baking pan. Spritz with cooking spray.

3. Bake 10 minutes. Remove from oven. Spread broccoli in a single layer along both sides of sheet pan (if broccoli is frozen, break pieces apart). Return to oven; bake 10 minutes longer. Remove from oven.

4. Preheat broiler. Spread marinara sauce over chicken; top with shredded cheese. Broil chicken and broccoli 3-4 in. from heat until cheese is golden brown and vegetables are tender, 3-5 minutes. If desired, sprinkle with basil.

|||||||||||

1 serving: 504 cal., 17g fat (7g sat. fat), 147mg chol., 1151mg sod., 27g carb. (10g sugars, 8g fiber), 52g pro.

Easy Addition: *Try serving this on a bed of riced cauliflower. A number of brands are available in the vegetable section of the freezer case.*

SHEET-PAN PINEAPPLE
CHICKEN FAJITAS

||||||||||||||||||||||||||||||||||||

For our fajitas, I combine chicken and pineapple for a different flavor. These fajitas are more on the sweet side, but my family just loves them!
—Nancy Heishman, Las Vegas, NV

PREP: 20 MIN.
COOK: 20 MIN.
MAKES: 6 SERVINGS

- 2 **Tbsp. coconut oil, melted**
- 3 **tsp. chili powder**
- 2 **tsp. ground cumin**
- 1 **tsp. garlic powder**
- ¾ **tsp. kosher salt**
- 1½ **lbs. chicken tenderloins, halved lengthwise**
- 1 **large red or sweet onion, halved and sliced (about 2 cups)**
- 1 **large sweet red pepper, cut into ½-in. strips**
- 1 **large green pepper, cut into ½-in. strips**
- 1 **Tbsp. minced seeded jalapeno pepper**
- 2 **cans (8 oz. each) unsweetened pineapple tidbits, drained**
- 2 **Tbsp. honey**
- 2 **Tbsp. lime juice**
- 12 **corn tortillas (6 in.), warmed**
  Optional: Pico de gallo, sour cream, shredded Mexican cheese blend, sliced avocado and lime wedges

1. Preheat oven to 425°. In a large bowl, mix first 5 ingredients; stir in chicken. Add onion, peppers, pineapple, honey and lime juice; toss to combine. Spread evenly in 2 greased 15x10x1-in. baking pans.

2. Roast 10 minutes, rotating pans halfway through cooking. Remove pans from oven; preheat broiler.

3. Broil chicken mixture, 1 pan at a time, 3-4 in. from heat until vegetables are lightly browned and chicken is no longer pink, 3-5 minutes. Serve in tortillas, with toppings and lime wedges as desired.

||||||||||||

2 fajitas: 359 cal., 8g fat (4g sat. fat), 56mg chol., 372mg sod., 45g carb. (19g sugars, 6g fiber), 31g pro. Diabetic exchanges: 3 starch, 3 lean meat, 1 fat.

Kitchen-Staple Swap: *If you don't have coconut oil on hand, substitute with canola or vegetable oil.*

SWISS CHICKEN
SLIDERS

|||||||||||||||||||||||||||||||||||||

*Friends came over for a
spur-of-the-moment bonfire,
and I dreamed up these quick
chicken sliders so we'd have
something to eat. Bake them
till the cheese is gooey.*
—Sara Martin, Whitefish, MT

TAKES: 25 MIN.
MAKES: 6 SERVINGS

- ½ cup mayonnaise
- 3 Tbsp. yellow mustard
- 12 mini buns, split
- 12 slices deli ham
- 3 cups shredded
rotisserie chicken
- 6 slices Swiss cheese,
cut in half

1. Preheat oven to 350°. In a small bowl, mix mayonnaise and mustard. Spread bun bottoms and tops with the mayonnaise mixture. Layer bottoms with ham, chicken and cheese; replace tops. Arrange in a single layer in a 15x10x1-in. baking pan.

2. Bake, covered, until sandwiches are heated through and cheese is melted, 10-15 minutes .

|||||||||||||||

*2 sliders: 508 cal., 27g fat (6g sat. fat), 100mg chol.,
894mg sod., 28g carb. (4g sugars, 1g fiber), 37g pro.*

SHEET-PAN
TANDOORI
CHICKEN

IIIIIIIIIIIIIIIIIIIIIIIIIIIIIIIIIIIIIII

This savory chicken recipe is easy for weeknights since it bakes in one pan, but it is also special enough for guests. The best part? There isn't much to clean up when dinner is over!
—Anwar Khan, Iriving, TX

PREP: 20 MIN. + MARINATING
BAKE: 25 MIN.
MAKES: 4 SERVINGS

- 1 cup plain Greek yogurt
- 3 Tbsp. tandoori masala seasoning
- ⅛ to ¼ tsp. crushed red pepper flakes, optional
- 8 bone-in chicken thighs (about 3 lbs.), skin removed
- 2 medium sweet potatoes, peeled and cut into ½-in. wedges
- 1 Tbsp. olive oil
- 16 cherry tomatoes
  Lemon slices
  Optional: Minced fresh cilantro and naan flatbreads

1. In a large bowl, whisk the yogurt, tandoori seasoning and, if desired, pepper flakes until blended. Add chicken and turn to coat. Cover and refrigerate 6-8 hours, turning occasionally.

2. Preheat oven to 450°. Drain chicken, discarding marinade in bowl. Place chicken in a greased 15x10x1-in. baking pan. Add sweet potatoes; drizzle with oil. Bake 15 minutes. Add tomatoes and lemon slices. Bake until a thermometer inserted into the chicken reads 170°-175°, 10-15 minutes longer. Broil 4-5 in. from the heat until browned, 4-5 minutes. If desired, serve with cilantro and naan.

IIIIIIIIIIIII

2 chicken thighs with 1 cup sweet potatoes and 4 tomatoes: 589 cal., 27g fat (9g sat. fat), 186mg chol., 187mg sod., 29g carb. (13g sugars, 6g fiber), 52g pro.

RANCH-MARINATED
CHICKEN BREASTS

‖‖‖‖‖‖‖‖‖‖‖‖‖‖‖‖‖‖‖‖‖‖‖‖‖‖‖‖‖‖‖‖‖

The pub-favorite pairing of ranch dressing and chicken comes home to your kitchen. With a little prep time the night before, you can have these savory chicken breasts ready in about half an hour.
—Barbee Decker, Whispering Pines, NC

PREP: 10 MIN. + MARINATING
BAKE: 25 MIN.
MAKES: 6 SERVINGS

- 2 **cups sour cream**
- 1 **envelope ranch salad dressing mix**
- 4 **tsp. lemon juice**
- 4 **tsp. Worcestershire sauce**
- 2 **tsp. celery salt**
- 2 **tsp. paprika**
- 1 **tsp. garlic salt**
- 1 **tsp. pepper**
- 6 **boneless skinless chicken breast halves (6 oz. each)**
- ¼ **cup butter, melted**

1. Combine the first 8 ingredients in a large shallow dish. Add chicken; turn to coat. Refrigerate, covered, 8 hours or overnight.

2. Drain chicken, discarding marinade. Place chicken in a greased 15x10x1-in. baking pan. Drizzle with butter. Bake, uncovered, at 350° for 25-30 minutes or until a thermometer reads 165°.

‖‖‖‖‖‖‖‖‖‖‖‖

1 chicken breast half : 421 cal., 28g fat (15g sat. fat), 133mg chol., 733mg sod., 5g carb. (3g sugars, 0 fiber), 37g pro.

GARLICKY CHICKEN DINNER

||||||||||||||||||||||||||||||

Flavorful bone-in chicken is enhanced by herbs, lemon and hearty vegetables in this savory meal-in-one entree.
—Shannon Norris, Cudahy, WI

PREP: 25 MIN.
BAKE: 45 MIN.
MAKES: 8 SERVINGS

- 1¼ **lbs. small red potatoes, quartered**
- 4 **medium carrots, cut into ½-in. slices**
- 1 **medium red onion, cut into thin wedges**
- 1 **Tbsp. olive oil**
- 6 **garlic cloves, minced**
- 2 **tsp. minced fresh thyme, divided**
- 1½ **tsp. salt, divided**
- 1 **tsp. pepper, divided**
- 1 **tsp. paprika**
- 4 **chicken drumsticks**
- 4 **bone-in chicken thighs**
- 1 **small lemon, sliced**
- 1 **pkg. (5 oz.) fresh spinach**

1. Preheat oven to 425°. In a large bowl, combine potatoes, carrots, onion, oil, garlic, 1 tsp. thyme, ¾ tsp. salt and ½ tsp. pepper; toss to coat. Transfer to a 15x10x1-in. baking pan coated with cooking spray.

2. In a small bowl, mix paprika and the remaining thyme, salt and pepper. Sprinkle chicken with paprika mixture; arrange over the vegetables. Top with lemon slices. Roast until a thermometer inserted in the chicken reads 170°-175° and vegetables are just tender, 35-40 minutes.

3. Remove chicken to a serving platter; keep warm. Top the vegetables with spinach. Roast until vegetables are tender and spinach is wilted, 8-10 minutes longer. Stir vegetables to combine; serve with chicken.

|||||||||||

1 piece chicken with 1 cup vegetables: 264 cal., 12g fat (3g sat. fat), 64mg chol., 548mg sod., 18g carb. (3g sugars, 3g fiber), 21g pro. Diabetic exchanges: 3 medium-fat meat, 1 starch, 1 vegetable, ½ fat.

TURKEY LATTICE
POPIE

||||||||||||||||||||||||||||||||||

With its pretty lattice crust, this cheesy dish is as appealing as it is tasty. It's easy to make, too, since it uses ready-to-go crescent roll dough.

—Lorraine Naig, Emmetsburg, IA

PREP: 20 MIN.
BAKE: 20 MIN.
MAKES: 12 SERVINGS

- 3 **tubes (8 oz. each) refrigerated crescent rolls**
- 4 **cups cubed cooked turkey**
- 1½ **cups shredded cheddar or Swiss cheese**
- 3 **cups frozen chopped broccoli, thawed and drained**
- 1 **can (10¾ oz.) condensed cream of chicken soup, undiluted**
- 1⅓ **cups 2% milk**
- 2 **Tbsp. Dijon mustard**
- 1 **Tbsp. dried minced onion**
- ½ **tsp. salt**
  Dash pepper
- 1 **large egg, lightly beaten**

1. Preheat oven to 375°. Unroll 2 tubes of crescent roll dough; separate into rectangles. Place the rectangles in an ungreased 15x10x1-in. baking pan. Press onto the bottom and ¼ in. up the sides of pan to form a crust, sealing seams and perforations. Bake 5-7 minutes or until light golden brown.

2. Meanwhile, in a large bowl, combine turkey, cheese, broccoli, soup, milk, mustard, onion, salt and pepper. Spoon over crust.

3. Unroll the remaining dough; divide into rectangles. Seal perforations. Cut each rectangle into four 1-in. strips. Using strips, make a lattice design on top of turkey mixture. Brush with egg. Bake 17-22 minutes or until the top crust is golden brown and filling is bubbly.

|||||||||||||

1 piece: 396 cal., 20g fat (4g sat. fat), 81mg chol., 934mg sod., 30g carb. (8g sugars, 2g fiber), 24g pro.

READER REVIEW
"I used a rotisserie chicken from the store since I didn't have turkey. We fed 10 fifth and sixth grade girls after a Bible study. Everyone enjoyed it, and that's a miracle!"
—RICH, TASTEOFHOME.COM

PARMESAN CHICKEN WITH
ARTICHOKE HEARTS

||||||||||||||||||||||||||||||||

I've liked the chicken and artichoke combo for a long time. Here's my own lemony twist. With all the praise it gets, this dinner is always so much fun to serve.
—Carly Giles, Ephraim, UT

PREP: 20 MIN.
BAKE: 20 MIN.
MAKES: 4 SERVINGS

- 4 boneless skinless chicken breast halves (6 oz. each)
- 3 tsp. olive oil, divided
- 1 tsp. dried rosemary, crushed
- ½ tsp. dried thyme
- ½ tsp. pepper
- 2 cans (14 oz. each) water-packed artichoke hearts, drained and quartered
- 1 medium onion, coarsely chopped
- ½ cup white wine or reduced-sodium chicken broth
- 2 garlic cloves, chopped
- ¼ cup shredded Parmesan cheese
- 1 lemon, cut into 8 slices
- 2 green onions, thinly sliced

1. Preheat oven to 375°. Place chicken in a 15x10x1-in. baking pan coated with cooking spray; drizzle with 1½ tsp. oil. In a small bowl, mix rosemary, thyme and pepper; sprinkle half over chicken.

2. In a large bowl, combine artichoke hearts, onion, wine, garlic, remaining oil and remaining herb mixture; toss to coat. Arrange around chicken. Sprinkle chicken with cheese; top with the lemon slices.

3. Roast until a thermometer inserted in chicken reads 165°, 20-25 minutes. Sprinkle with green onions.

|||||||||||||

1 chicken breast half with ¾ cup artichoke mixture: 339 cal., 9g fat (3g sat. fat), 98mg chol., 667mg sod., 18g carb. (2g sugars, 1g fiber), 42g pro. Diabetic exchanges: 5 lean meat, 1 vegetable, 1 fat, ½ starch.

HOT & SPICY
TURKEY LEGS

IIIIIIIIIIIIIIIIIIIIIIIIIIIIII

Why wait for the next fair when you can make incredible turkey legs at home? Grab a handful of seasonings and get ready for a flavor explosion at dinner!
—*Taste of Home* Test Kitchen

PREP: 10 MIN. + MARINATING
BAKE: 1½ HOURS
MAKES: 4 SERVINGS

- 4 **turkey drumsticks (1½ lbs. each)**
- ⅔ **cup Louisiana-style hot sauce**
- ⅓ **cup canola oil**
- 1 **Tbsp. reduced-sodium soy sauce**
- 1 **Tbsp. chili powder**
- 2 **tsp. ground mustard**
- 1 **tsp. garlic powder**
- 1 **tsp. poultry seasoning**
- 1 **tsp. onion powder**
- 1 **tsp. celery salt**
- ½ **tsp. white pepper**
- ½ **tsp. hot pepper sauce, optional**

1. Divide drumsticks between 2 large bowls or shallow dishes. In a smaller bowl, whisk remaining ingredients until blended. Add ¾ cup marinade to drumsticks, dividing evenly between the bowls. Turn to coat. Cover and refrigerate 8 hours or overnight. Cover and refrigerate remaining marinade.

2. Preheat oven to 375°. Remove drumsticks from marinade to a foil-lined 15x10x1-in. baking pan; discard marinade in bowls.

3. Bake, covered, 45 minutes. Uncover; bake 45-60 minutes longer or until a thermometer reads 175°, basting occasionally with reserved marinade.

IIIIIIIIIIII

1 turkey drumstick: 937 cal., 50g fat (13g sat. fat), 343mg chol., 587mg sod., 2g carb. (1g sugars, 1g fiber), 113g pro.

CHICKEN
PROVOLONE

IIIIIIIIIIIIIIIIIIIIIIIIIIIIIIII

Chicken Provolone, though one of my simplest dishes, is one of my husband's favorites. It is easy to prepare and looks fancy with a garnish of fresh parsley or basil. Add some buttered noodles for an easy side dish.
—Dawn Bryant, Thedford, NE

TAKES: 25 MIN.
MAKES: 4 SERVINGS

- 4 boneless skinless chicken breast halves (4 oz. each)
- ¼ tsp. pepper Butter-flavored cooking spray
- 8 fresh basil leaves
- 4 thin slices prosciutto or deli ham
- 4 slices provolone cheese

1. Sprinkle chicken with pepper. In a large skillet coated with cooking spray, cook chicken over medium heat until a thermometer reads 165°, 4-5 minutes on each side.

2. Transfer to an ungreased baking sheet; top with the basil, prosciutto and cheese. Broil 6-8 in. from the heat until cheese is melted, 1-2 minutes.

IIIIIIIIIIII

1 chicken breast half: 236 cal., 11g fat (6g sat. fat), 89mg chol., 435mg sod., 1g carb. (0 sugars, 0 fiber), 33g pro. Diabetic exchanges: 4 lean meat.

CREAMY CHICKEN
ENCHILADA PIZZA

IIIIIIIIIIIIIIIIIIIIIIIIIIIIIIIII

*This is a twist on a family
favorite. We wanted the taste
of my chicken enchilada recipe,
but we wanted it even faster.
This kicked-up pizza is the fun
creation we came up with.*
—Crystal Jo Bruns, Iliff, CO

TAKES: 30 MIN.
MAKES: 6 SERVINGS

- 1   **tube (11 oz.) refrigerated thin pizza crust**
- 1   **pkg. (8 oz.) cream cheese, softened, cubed**
- 1   **cup shredded Mexican cheese blend, divided**
- 2   **tsp. ground cumin**
- 1½ **tsp. garlic powder**
- ½   **tsp. salt**
- 2   **cups ready-to-use fajita chicken strips, cubed**
- ½   **cup salsa**
- ¼   **cup green enchilada sauce**
  Optional toppings: Shredded lettuce, chopped tomatoes and sliced ripe olives

1. Preheat oven to 400°. Unroll and press dough onto bottom and ½ in. up sides of a greased 15x10x1-in. baking pan. Bake 5 minutes.

2. Meanwhile, in a small saucepan, combine cream cheese, ½ cup cheese, cumin, garlic powder and salt over medium heat; cook and stir for 5 minutes or until blended. Remove from heat. Add chicken; toss to coat.

3. Spread over crust. Drizzle with salsa and enchilada sauce; sprinkle with remaining cheese. Bake until crust is golden and cheese is melted, 8-12 minutes longer. Serve with toppings of your choice.

IIIIIIIIIIII

1 piece: 428 cal., 25g fat (12g sat. fat), 83mg chol., 1061mg sod., 30g carb. (5g sugars, 1g fiber), 20g pro.

Just a Note: *The super creamy topping on this pizza will prevent the bottom of the crust from crisping up as much as a traditional pizza.*

QUICK & EASY
STROMBOLI

||||||||||||||||||||||||||||||||||||

Sandwich fixings get rolled into this dinner favorite, thanks to refrigerated pizza dough. Use any combo of cheese, deli meat and veggies that you like or whatever you have on hand.
—Catherine Cassidy, Milwaukee, WI

TAKES: 30 MIN.
MAKES: 8 SERVINGS

- 1   tube (13.8 oz.) refrigerated pizza crust
- ½   lb. thinly sliced deli turkey
- ½   lb. thinly sliced Muenster cheese
- ¼   cup pickled pepper rings
- 2   tsp. yellow mustard
- 2   tsp. minced fresh herbs or ½ tsp. dried herbs
- 1   large egg
- 1   Tbsp. water

1. Preheat oven to 350°. Unroll pizza dough onto the bottom of a greased 15x10x1-in. baking pan. Layer with turkey, cheese and peppers. Spread with mustard; sprinkle with herbs.

2. Roll dough into a log; pinch ends to seal. In a small bowl, combine egg and water; brush over dough. Bake until crust is lightly browned, 20-25 minutes. Slice and serve.

|||||||||||||

1 piece: 271 cal., 11g fat (6g sat. fat), 42mg chol., 965mg sod., 25g carb. (3g sugars, 1g fiber), 19g pro.

SHEET-PAN
HONEY MUSTARD CHICKEN

IIIIIIIIIIIIIIIIIIIIIIIIIIIIIIIIIIIII

This sheet-pan chicken is an easy gluten-free, low-carb meal ideal for busy weekdays. The chicken is tender, juicy and so delicious! It made the list of our favorite meals. You can substitute any low-carb vegetable for green beans.
—Denise Browning, San Antonio, TX

PREP: 20 MIN.
BAKE: 40 MIN.
MAKES: 6 SERVINGS

- 6 **bone-in chicken thighs** (about 2¼ lbs.)
- ¾ **tsp. salt, divided**
- ½ **tsp. pepper, divided**
- 2 **medium lemons**
- ⅓ **cup olive oil**
- ⅓ **cup honey**
- 3 **Tbsp. Dijon mustard**
- 4 **garlic cloves, minced**
- 1 **tsp. paprika**
- ½ **cup water**
- ½ **lb. fresh green beans, trimmed**
- 6 **miniature sweet peppers, sliced into rings**
- ¼ **cup pomegranate seeds, optional**

1. Preheat oven to 425°. Place chicken in a greased 15x10x1-in. baking pan. Sprinkle with ½ tsp. salt and ¼ tsp. pepper. Thinly slice 1 lemon; place over chicken. Cut the remaining lemon crosswise in half; squeeze juice into a small bowl. Whisk in oil, honey, mustard, garlic and paprika. Pour half the sauce over chicken; reserve remaining for beans. Pour water into pan. Bake 25 minutes.

2. Meanwhile, combine beans, sweet peppers, remaining sauce, ¼ tsp. salt and ¼ tsp. pepper; toss to coat. Arrange vegetables around chicken in pan. Bake until a thermometer inserted in chicken reads 170°-175° and beans are tender, 15-20 minutes. If desired, sprinkle with pomegranate seeds.

IIIIIIIIIIIII

1 serving: 419 cal., 26g fat (6g sat. fat), 81mg chol., 548mg sod., 22g carb. (17g sugars, 2g fiber), 24g pro.

PORK
SUPPERS

||||||||||||||||||

BACON, LETTUCE &
TOMATO PIZZA

IIIIIIIIIIIIIIIIIIIIIIIIIIIIIIIIII

*I combine two all-time favorites
in this recipe: pizza and BLT
sandwiches. I brought this
fun mashup to a ladies lunch
and was met with lots of oohs
and aahs.*
—Bonnie Hawkins, Elkhorn, WI

TAKES: 30 MIN.
MAKES: 6 SERVINGS

- 1   tube (13.8 oz.)
      refrigerated pizza crust
- 2   Tbsp. olive oil
- 2   Tbsp. grated
      Parmesan cheese
- 1   tsp. garlic salt
- ½   cup mayonnaise
- 2   tsp. ranch dip mix
- 4   cups shredded romaine
- 3   to 4 plum tomatoes,
      chopped
- ½   lb. bacon strips,
      cooked and crumbled

1. Preheat oven to 425°. Unroll and press dough onto bottom
of a greased 15x10x1-in. baking pan. Brush with oil; top with the
cheese and garlic salt. Bake until golden brown, 15-18 minutes;
cool slightly.

2. Meanwhile, combine mayonnaise and ranch dip mix. Spread
over pizza crust; top with romaine, tomatoes and bacon.

IIIIIIIIIIIII

*1 serving: 389 cal., 23g fat (5g sat. fat), 16mg chol.,
1236mg sod., 34g carb. (5g sugars, 2g fiber), 11g pro.*

*Kick Things up a Notch: Amp up the flavor of this pizza
by adding a bit of torn fresh basil with the romaine.*

MEMPHIS-STYLE
BBQ RIBS

|||||||||||||||||||||||||||||||||||||||||

A friend of mine who loves barbecue gave me her recipe for ribs. Use just enough of the spice mixture to rub over them before baking, and sprinkle on the rest later.
—Jennifer Ross, Arlington, TN

PREP: 20 MIN.
BAKE: 3½ HOURS
MAKES: 6 SERVINGS

- ¼ cup packed brown sugar
- ¼ cup paprika
- 2 Tbsp. kosher salt
- 2 Tbsp. onion powder
- 2 Tbsp. garlic powder
- 2 Tbsp. coarsely ground pepper
- 3 racks (1½ to 2 lbs. each) pork baby back ribs
  Barbecue sauce, optional

1. Preheat oven to 350°. In a bowl, mix the first 6 ingredients; rub ¾ cup over ribs. Wrap rib racks in large pieces of heavy-duty foil; seal tightly. Place in a 15x10x1-in. baking pan. Bake 1½ hours. Reduce oven setting to 250°. Bake until tender, 1½ hours longer.

2. Carefully remove the ribs from foil; return to baking pan. Sprinkle ribs with remaining spice mixture. Bake 30 minutes longer or until lightly browned, brushing with barbecue sauce, if desired.

|||||||||||||

1 serving: 497 cal., 32g fat (11g sat. fat), 122mg chol., 2066mg sod., 17g carb. (10g sugars, 3g fiber), 35g pro.

ALMOND PORK CHOPS WITH
HONEY MUSTARD

||||||||||||||||||||||||||||||||||||

I love how crunchy almonds and sweet mustard jazz up this tender main course. I double the recipe because one chop per person is never enough for my crowd of grown children and grandkids.
—Lily Julow, Lawrenceville, GA

TAKES: 30 MIN.
MAKES: 4 SERVINGS

- ½ cup smoked almonds
- ½ cup dry bread crumbs
- 2 large eggs
- ⅓ cup all-purpose flour
- ¼ tsp. salt
- ⅛ tsp. pepper
- 4 boneless pork loin chops (1 in. thick and 6 oz. each)
- 2 Tbsp. olive oil
- 2 Tbsp. butter
- ½ cup reduced-fat mayonnaise
- ¼ cup honey
- 2 Tbsp. Dijon mustard

1. In a food processor, process the almonds until finely chopped. Transfer to a shallow bowl; add bread crumbs. In another bowl, beat the eggs. In a large bowl, combine flour, salt and pepper. Add 1 pork chop at a time and toss to coat. Dip pork chop in eggs, then coat with almond mixture.

2. Preheat oven to 400°. In a large skillet over medium heat, cook chops in oil and butter until lightly browned, 2-3 minutes on each side. Transfer pork chops to a rimmed baking sheet; bake, uncovered, until a thermometer inserted in pork reads 145°, 10-15 minutes. Meanwhile, in a small bowl, combine mayonnaise, honey and mustard. Serve with pork chops.

||||||||||||

1 pork chop with about 3 Tbsp. sauce: 642 cal., 40g fat (11g sat. fat), 204mg chol., 659mg sod., 31g carb. (20g sugars, 2g fiber), 39g pro.

BLT MEATBALL
SLIDERS

IIIIIIIIIIIIIIIIIIIIIIIIIIIIIIIIIIIIIII

Take sliders to a whole new level with the addition of bacon, ground pork and zesty ranch mayo. Your guests will surely make these disappear fast.
—Damali Campbell, New York, NY

PREP: 25 MIN.
BAKE: 30 MIN.
MAKES: 1½ DOZEN

- 1 lb. uncooked bacon strips
- 1 cup 2% milk
- 1 large egg
- 1 cup dry bread crumbs
- 1 small onion, finely chopped
- 1 Tbsp. fennel seed, crushed
- 1 tsp. salt
- 1 tsp. pepper
- ½ tsp. crushed red pepper flakes
- ¾ lb. ground pork
- ½ lb. lean ground beef (90% lean)
- ⅔ cup mayonnaise
- 1½ tsp. ranch dip mix
- 18 dinner rolls, split
- 3 cups spring mix salad greens
- 3 plum tomatoes, sliced

1. Place bacon in a food processor; cover and process until finely chopped. In a large bowl, combine the milk, egg, bread crumbs, onion and seasonings. Crumble the bacon, pork and beef over mixture and mix well. Shape into 2-in. meatballs.

2. Place in an ungreased 15x10x1-in. baking pan. Bake at 425° for 30-35 minutes or until a thermometer reads 160°.

3. Combine mayonnaise and dip mix; spread on roll tops. Layer each roll bottom with salad greens, a tomato slice and a meatball; replace tops.

IIIIIIIIIIII

1 slider: 384 cal., 25g fat (7g sat. fat), 71mg chol., 691mg sod., 25g carb. (3g sugars, 2g fiber), 14g pro.

LEMON-DIJON PORK
SHEET-PAN SUPPER

||||||||||||||||||||||||||||||||

Most nights I need something on the table with minimal effort and maximum results. This sheet-pan supper has become an all-time favorite, not only because of its bright flavors but also because of its speedy cleanup time!
—Elisabeth Larsen, Pleasant Grove, UT

PREP: 20 MIN.
BAKE: 20 MIN.
MAKES: 4 SERVINGS

- 4 tsp. Dijon mustard
- 2 tsp. grated lemon zest
- 1 garlic clove, minced
- ½ tsp. salt
- 2 Tbsp. canola oil
- 1½ lbs. sweet potatoes (about 3 medium), cut into ½-in. cubes
- 1 lb. fresh Brussels sprouts (about 4 cups), quartered
- 4 boneless pork loin chops (6 oz. each) Coarsely ground pepper, optional

1. Preheat oven to 425°. In a large bowl, mix first 4 ingredients; gradually whisk in oil. Reserve 1 Tbsp. mixture. Add vegetables to remaining mixture; toss to coat.

2. Place pork chops and vegetables in a 15x10x1-in. pan coated with cooking spray. Brush the chops with the reserved mustard mixture. Roast 10 minutes.

3. Turn chops and stir vegetables; roast until a thermometer inserted in the pork reads 145° and vegetables are tender, 10-15 minutes longer. If desired, sprinkle with pepper. Let stand 5 minutes before serving.

||||||||||||||

1 pork chop with 1¼ cups vegetables: 516 cal., 17g fat (4g sat. fat), 82mg chol., 505mg sod., 51g carb. (19g sugars, 9g fiber), 39g pro. Diabetic exchanges: 5 lean meat, 3 starch, 1½ fat, 1 vegetable.

Chop, Chop: If you cut the Brussels sprouts and potatoes fairly small, they'll be perfectly tender by the time the pork is cooked.

ROASTED KIELBASA
& VEGETABLES

||||||||||||||||||||||||||||||||||

*The first reason I enjoy this
dish is because it's so hearty.
Second, it is a one-pan meal.
That's a win-win dinner!*
—Marietta Slater, Justin, TX

PREP: 20 MIN.
BAKE: 40 MIN.
MAKES: 6 SERVINGS

- 3 medium sweet potatoes,
     peeled and cut into
     1-in. pieces
- 1 large sweet onion,
     cut into 1-in. pieces
- 4 medium carrots,
     cut into 1-in. pieces
- 2 Tbsp. olive oil
- 1 lb. smoked kielbasa or
     Polish sausage, halved
     and cut into 1-in. pieces
- 1 medium yellow
     summer squash,
     cut into 1-in. pieces
- 1 medium zucchini,
     cut into 1-in. pieces
- ¼ tsp. salt
- ¼ tsp. pepper
     Dijon mustard, optional

1. Preheat oven to 400°. Divide sweet potatoes, onion and carrots between 2 greased 15x10x1-in. baking pans. Drizzle with oil; toss to coat. Roast 25 minutes, stirring occasionally.

2. Add kielbasa, squash and zucchini to pans; sprinkle with salt and pepper. Roast until vegetables are tender, 15-20 minutes longer. Transfer to a serving bowl; toss to combine. If desired, serve with mustard.

|||||||||||||

1⅔ cups: 378 cal., 25g fat (8g sat. fat), 51mg chol., 954mg sod., 26g carb. (12g sugars, 4g fiber), 13g pro.

HAM & PINEAPPLE
KABOBS

|||||||||||||||||||||||||||||||||||

*My family turns ham and
pineapple into juicy kabobs.
The marinade gets its unique
zip from a combo of hoisin,
teriyaki and soy sauces.*
—Chandra Lane Sirois, Kansas City, MO

PREP: 30 MIN. + MARINATING
BAKE: 15 MIN.
MAKES: 12 SERVINGS

- ¼ cup hoisin sauce
- ¼ cup unsweetened
  pineapple juice
- ¼ cup teriyaki sauce
- 1 Tbsp. honey
- 1½ tsp. rice vinegar
- 1½ tsp. reduced-sodium
  soy sauce
- 2 lbs. fully cooked
  boneless ham,
  cut into 1-in. pieces
- 1 large fresh pineapple,
  peeled, cored and
  cut into 1-in. cubes
  (about 4 cups)

1. In a large shallow dish, combine the first 6 ingredients. Add ham; turn to coat. Refrigerate, covered, overnight.

2. Preheat oven to 350°. Drain ham, reserving marinade. For glaze, pour marinade into a small saucepan; bring to a boil. Reduce heat; simmer, uncovered, 5-7 minutes or until slightly thickened, stirring occasionally. Remove from heat.

3. Meanwhile, on 12 metal or soaked wooden skewers, alternately thread ham and pineapple; place in a foil-lined 15x10x1-in. baking pan. Brush with glaze. Bake, uncovered, 15-20 minutes or until lightly browned.

||||||||||||||

*1 kabob: 144 cal., 3g fat (1g sat. fat), 39mg chol.,
1109mg sod., 15g carb. (12g sugars, 1g fiber), 15g pro.*

*Make & Take: Consider doubling this recipe when you
need a savory contribution to a party or potluck. The
kabobs travel well and make a perfect change-of-pace
addition to buffet tables.*

SPICY ROASTED
SAUSAGE, POTATOES & PEPPERS

||||||||||||||||||||||||||||||||||

I love to share food, and this hearty meal-in-one has gotten a savory reputation around town. People have actually approached me in public to ask for the recipe.
—Laurie Sledge, Brandon, MS

PREP: 20 MIN.
BAKE: 30 MIN.
MAKES: 4 SERVINGS

1   lb. potatoes
    (about 2 medium),
    peeled and cut into
    ½-in. cubes
1   pkg. (12 oz.) fully cooked
    andouille chicken
    sausage links or
    flavor of your choice,
    cut into 1-in. pieces
1   medium red onion,
    cut into wedges
1   medium sweet
    red pepper,
    cut into 1-in. pieces
1   medium green pepper,
    cut into 1-in. pieces
½   cup pickled pepper rings
1   Tbsp. olive oil
½   to 1 tsp. Creole
    seasoning
¼   tsp. pepper

1. Preheat oven to 400°. In a large bowl, combine potatoes, sausage, onion, red pepper, green pepper and pepper rings. Mix oil, Creole seasoning and pepper; drizzle over potato mixture and toss to coat.

2. Transfer to a 15x10x1-in. baking pan coated with cooking spray. Roast until vegetables are tender, stirring occasionally, 30-35 minutes.

|||||||||||||

1½ cups: 257 cal., 11g fat (3g sat. fat), 65mg chol., 759mg sod., 24g carb. (5g sugars, 3g fiber), 17g pro. Diabetic exchanges: 3 lean meat, 1 starch, 1 vegetable, 1 fat.

BAKED HAM & COLBY SANDWICHES

||||||||||||||||||||||||||||||||

This yummy recipe is a winner with our friends and family. Not only are the warm sandwiches a snap to prepare, but they smell so good when they are baking that no one is able to resist them. They're a staple at our get-togethers.
—Sherry Crenshaw, Fort Worth, TX

TAKES: 30 MIN.
MAKES: 8 SANDWICHES

- ½ cup butter, melted
- 2 Tbsp. prepared mustard
- 1 Tbsp. dried minced onion
- 1 Tbsp. poppy seeds
- 2 to 3 tsp. sugar
- 8 hamburger buns, split
- 8 slices Colby cheese
- 16 thin slices deli ham (about 1 lb.)
- 1½ cups shredded part-skim mozzarella cheese

1. In a small bowl, combine the butter, mustard, onion, poppy seeds and sugar. Place the bun bottoms, cut side up, in an ungreased 15x10x1-in. baking pan. Top each with Colby cheese, ham and mozzarella. Brush with half the butter mixture.

2. Replace bun tops. Brush with the remaining butter mixture. Bake, uncovered, at 350° until cheese is melted, 10-15 minutes.

||||||||||||||

1 sandwich: 504 cal., 32g fat (18g sat. fat), 102mg chol., 1444mg sod., 27g carb. (5g sugars, 1g fiber), 27g pro.

Say Cheese: Feel free to substitute your favorite cheeses into these sandwiches, such as swapping Colby with cheddar.

PORK & ASPARAGUS
SHEET-PAN DINNER

||||||||||||||||||||||||||||||||||||

When time is of the essence, it's nice to have a quick and easy meal idea in your back pocket. This meal-in-one dish is delicious and can be cleaned up in a flash.
—Joan Hallford, North Richland Hills, TX

PREP: 20 MIN.
BAKE: 20 MIN.
MAKES: 4 SERVINGS

- ¼ cup olive oil, divided
- 3 cups diced new potatoes
- 3 cups cut fresh asparagus (1-in. pieces)
- ¼ tsp. salt
- ¼ tsp. pepper
- 1 large gala or Honeycrisp apple, peeled and cut into 1-in. wedges
- 2 tsp. brown sugar
- 1 tsp. ground cinnamon
- ¼ tsp. ground ginger
- 4 boneless pork loin chops (1 in. thick and about 6 oz. each)
- 2 tsp. Southwest seasoning

1. Preheat oven to 425°. Line a 15x10x1-in. baking pan with foil; brush with 2 tsp. olive oil.

2. In a large bowl, toss potatoes with 1 Tbsp. olive oil. Place in 1 section of prepared baking pan. In same bowl, toss the asparagus with 1 Tbsp. olive oil; place in another section of pan. Sprinkle salt and pepper over potatoes and asparagus.

3. In same bowl, toss apple with 1 tsp. olive oil. In a small bowl, mix brown sugar, cinnamon and ginger; sprinkle over apples and toss to coat. Transfer to a different section of pan.

4. Brush the pork chops with remaining olive oil; sprinkle both sides with Southwest seasoning. Place the chops in remaining section of pan. Bake until a thermometer inserted in pork reads 145° and potatoes and apples are tender, 20-25 minutes. Let stand 5 minutes before serving.

|||||||||||||

1 serving: 486 cal., 23g fat (5g sat. fat), 82mg chol., 447mg sod., 32g carb. (10g sugars, 5g fiber), 37g pro.

BUSY-DAY
PORK CHOPS

|||||||||||||||||||||||||||||||

I created this recipe one day when I had pork chops and needed to find a simple way to make them. It was so easy and resulted in rave reviews! The chops are crispy outside, even though the preparation technique uses less fat.

—Dee Maltby, Wayne, OH

TAKES: 25 MIN.
MAKES: 4 SERVINGS

- ¼ cup fat-free milk
- ¼ cup seasoned bread crumbs
- ¼ cup grated Parmesan cheese
- ¼ tsp. salt
- ¼ tsp. garlic powder
- ⅛ tsp. pepper
- 4 boneless pork loin chops (4 oz. each)
  Cooking spray

1. Preheat oven to 375°. Place milk in a shallow bowl. In another shallow bowl, toss bread crumbs with cheese and seasonings.

2. Dip pork chops in milk, then coat with crumb mixture. Place on a baking sheet coated with cooking spray; lightly spritz the chops with cooking spray.

3. Bake 8-10 minutes on each side or until a thermometer reads 145°. Let stand 5 minutes before serving.

|||||||||||||

1 pork chop: 178 cal., 7g fat (3g sat. fat), 57mg chol., 207mg sod., 3g carb. (0 sugars, 0 fiber), 23g pro. Diabetic exchanges: 3 lean meat.

ORANGE-GLAZED PORK WITH
SWEET POTATOES

||||||||||||||||||||||||||||||||||||

When it's chilly outside, I like to roast pork tenderloin with sweet potatoes, apples and an orange. The sweetness and spices make any evening cozy.
—Danielle Lee Boyles, Weston, WI

PREP: 20 MIN.
BAKE: 55 MIN. + STANDING
MAKES: 6 SERVINGS

- 1 **lb. sweet potatoes (about 2 medium)**
- 2 **medium apples**
- 1 **medium orange**
- 1 **tsp. salt**
- ½ **tsp. pepper**
- 1 **cup orange juice**
- 2 **Tbsp. brown sugar**
- 2 **tsp. cornstarch**
- 1 **tsp. ground cinnamon**
- 1 **tsp. ground ginger**
- 2 **pork tenderloins (about 1 lb. each)**

1. Preheat oven to 350°. Peel sweet potatoes; core apples. Cut potatoes, apples and orange crosswise into ¼-in.-thick slices. Arrange in a foil-lined 15x10x1-in. baking pan coated with cooking spray; sprinkle with salt and pepper. Roast 10 minutes.

2. Meanwhile, in a microwave-safe bowl, mix orange juice, brown sugar, cornstarch, cinnamon and ginger. Microwave, covered, on high, stirring every 30 seconds until thickened, 1-2 minutes. Stir until smooth.

3. Place pork over sweet potato mixture; drizzle with orange juice mixture. Roast until a thermometer inserted in pork reads 145° and sweet potatoes and apples are tender, 45-55 minutes longer. Remove from oven; tent with foil. Let stand 10 minutes before slicing.

||||||||||||

4 oz. cooked pork with about 1 cup sweet potato mixture: 325 cal., 5g fat (2g sat. fat), 85mg chol., 467mg sod., 36g carb. (21g sugars, 3g fiber), 32g pro. Diabetic exchanges: 4 lean meat, 2 starch.

OVEN-FRIED
GREEN TOMATO BLT

||||||||||||||||||||||||||||||||

For years I have used this same idea to cook eggplant slices, and recently I decided to try it on green tomatoes. It worked! Now my family loves them in BLTs.
—Jolene Martinelli, Fremont, NH

TAKES: 25 MIN.
MAKES: 4 SERVINGS

- 1 **large green tomato (about 8 oz.)**
- 1 **large egg, beaten**
- 1 **cup panko bread crumbs**
- ¼ **tsp. salt**
- ¼ **cup reduced-fat mayonnaise**
- 2 **green onions, thinly sliced**
- 1 **tsp. snipped fresh dill or ¼ tsp. dill weed**
- 8 **slices whole wheat bread, toasted**
- 8 **cooked center-cut bacon strips**
- 4 **Bibb or Boston lettuce leaves**

1. Preheat broiler. Cut tomato into 8 slices, each about ¼ in. thick. Place egg and bread crumbs in separate shallow bowls; mix salt into bread crumbs. Dip tomato slices in egg, then in bread crumb mixture, patting to help adhere.

2. Place the tomato slices on a wire rack set in a 15x10x1-in. baking pan; broil 4-5 in. from heat until golden brown, about 30-45 seconds per side.

3. Mix mayonnaise, green onions and dill. Layer each of 4 slices of bread with 2 bacon strips, 1 lettuce leaf and 2 tomato slices. Spread mayonnaise mixture over remaining slices of bread; place over top layer.

|||||||||||||

1 sandwich: 313 cal., 12g fat (2g sat. fat), 55mg chol., 744mg sod., 36g carb. (5g sugars, 4g fiber), 16g pro. Diabetic exchanges: 2 starch, 2 high-fat meat, 1 fat.

Go Green: Green tomatoes are simply unripe tomatoes. They have a slight acidic bite to them, and they're a little crunchier than ripe tomatoes.

POTATO & PEPPER
SAUSAGE BAKE

||||||||||||||||||||||||||||||||||||

*When my family smells this
dish baking in the oven, they
know they are in for a treat! If
you like spice, add a pinch of
red pepper flakes or switch
the mild Italian sausage to
hot Italian sausage.*
—Ashli Claytor, Chesapeake, VA

PREP: 25 MIN.
BAKE: 30 MIN.
MAKES: 5 SERVINGS

- 5 large Yukon Gold potatoes, peeled and cut into 1-in. cubes
- 1 large sweet orange pepper, sliced
- 1 large sweet red pepper, sliced
- 1 shallot, chopped
- 4 garlic cloves, minced
- 1 Tbsp. olive oil
- 2 tsp. paprika
- ¾ tsp. salt
- ½ tsp. dried thyme
- ½ tsp. pepper
- 1 pkg. (19 oz.) Italian sausage links
  Minced fresh thyme, optional

1. Preheat oven to 400°. Place the potatoes, sweet peppers, shallot and garlic in a greased 15x10x1-in. baking pan. Drizzle with oil. Sprinkle with seasonings; toss to coat. Spread evenly over pan, leaving room for the sausage. Add sausage to pan.

2. Bake, uncovered, until a thermometer inserted in sausage reads 160° and vegetables are tender, 30-35 minutes. If desired, sprinkle with fresh thyme before serving.

||||||||||||||

1 sausage link with ¾ cup vegetables: 446 cal., 26g fat (8g sat. fat), 58mg chol., 1021mg sod., 38g carb. (5g sugars, 4g fiber), 16g pro.

Keep 'Em Separated: Arrange the sausages directly on the pan instead of on top of the potatoes, so the potatoes cook evenly.

HAM & CHEESE
STROMBOLI

IIIIIIIIIIIIIIIIIIIIIIIIIIIIIIIIII

I like to make several of these savory loaves to keep in the freezer for weeknight meals. Loaded with ham, broccoli and cheese, the spiral sandwich slices are ideal for folks with busy lifestyles.
—Susan Brown, Lithonia, GA

PREP: 15 MIN.
BAKE: 35 MIN. + STANDING
MAKES: 6 SERVINGS

- 1 loaf (1 lb.) frozen white bread dough, thawed
- ½ lb. sliced Swiss cheese
- ½ lb. thinly sliced deli ham
- 1 cup shredded cheddar cheese
- 1 cup shredded Colby cheese
- 1 pkg. (16 oz.) frozen chopped broccoli, thawed and drained
- ½ tsp. garlic powder

1. On a floured surface, roll dough into an 18x12-in. rectangle. Layer with Swiss cheese, ham, cheddar cheese, Colby cheese and broccoli to within 1 in. of edges; sprinkle with the garlic powder. Roll up jelly-roll style, starting with a long side; seal seams and ends.

2. Place seam side down on a greased 15x10x1-in. baking pan. Bake, uncovered, at 400° for 20 minutes. Cover loosely with foil; bake 15-20 minutes longer. Let stand for 10 minutes before slicing.

FREEZE OPTION: Freeze cooled baked Stromboli in heavy-duty foil. To use, remove from foil and place on a greased baking sheet in a preheated 350° oven until heated through.

IIIIIIIIIIII

1 slice: 583 cal., 30g fat (17g sat. fat), 100mg chol., 1256mg sod., 42g carb. (4g sugars, 5g fiber), 35g pro.

CIDER-GLAZED
PORK CHOPS
WITH CARROTS

||||||||||||||||||||||||||||||||||||

Treat the family to this pork chop dinner, and they'll think you took culinary classes. No one will ever guess that this simple main dish cost about $2 a serving!
—*Taste of Home* Test Kitchen

PREP: 20 MIN.
COOK: 15 MIN.
MAKES: 4 SERVINGS

- 4 **bone-in pork loin chops (7 oz. each)**
- 4 **tsp. olive oil, divided**
- ¾ **cup apple cider or juice**
- 2 **Tbsp. brown sugar**
- 2 **Tbsp. cider vinegar**
- 2 **Tbsp. soy sauce**
- 3 **garlic cloves, minced**
- 2 **tsp. prepared mustard**
- ½ **tsp. ground ginger**
- 8 **small carrots, halved lengthwise**
- ½ **tsp. salt**
- ¼ **tsp. pepper**

1. In a large skillet, brown pork chops on both sides in 3 tsp. oil.

2. In a small bowl, combine the cider, brown sugar, vinegar, soy sauce, garlic, mustard and ginger; pour over the chops. Bring to a boil. Reduce heat; cover and simmer for 15-20 minutes or until tender.

3. Meanwhile, place carrots in a greased 15x10x1-in. baking pan. Drizzle with remaining oil. Sprinkle with salt and pepper; toss to coat.

4. Bake, uncovered, at 425° for 15-20 minutes or until tender, turning once. Serve with pork chops.

|||||||||||||

1 serving: 326 cal., 13g fat (4g sat. fat), 63mg chol., 897mg sod., 23g carb. (16g sugars, 3g fiber), 28g pro.

SAUSAGE & PEPPER
SHEET-PAN SANDWICHES

||||||||||||||||||||||||||||||||

Sausage and peppers were always on the table when I was growing up. Here's how I do it the easy way: Just grab a sheet pan and the ingredients, then let the oven do the work.
—Debbie Glasscock, Conway, AR

PREP: 20 MIN.
BAKE: 30 MIN.
MAKES: 6 SERVINGS

- 1 lb. uncooked sweet Italian turkey sausage links, roughly chopped
- 3 medium sweet red peppers, seeded and sliced
- 1 large onion, halved and sliced
- 1 Tbsp. olive oil
- 6 hot dog buns, split
- 6 slices provolone cheese

1. Preheat oven to 375°. Place sausage pieces in a 15x10x1-in. sheet pan, arranging the peppers and onion around sausage. Drizzle olive oil over sausage and vegetables; bake, stirring mixture after 15 minutes, until the sausage is no longer pink and vegetables are tender, 30-35 minutes.

2. During the last 5 minutes of baking, arrange buns cut side up in a second sheet pan; top each bun bottom with a cheese slice. Bake until buns are golden brown and cheese is melted. Spoon sausage and pepper mixture onto bun bottoms. Replace tops.

|||||||||||||

1 sandwich: 315 cal., 15g fat (5g sat. fat), 43mg chol., 672mg sod., 28g carb. (7g sugars, 2g fiber), 18g p

Bigger & Better: For a family-sized sandwich, swap out the hot dog buns for a large loaf of French bread cut in half lengthwise.

PORK
SATAY

Cilantro gives this delightful dish freshness, while the sesame oil and Thai chili sauce add layers of Asian taste that pair perfectly with the flavor of peanut butter.
—*Taste of Home* Test Kitchen

PREP: 20 MIN. + MARINATING
COOK: 10 MIN.
MAKES: 20 SERVINGS

- ⅓   cup reduced-sodium soy sauce
- 2   green onions, sliced
- 3   Tbsp. brown sugar
- 3   Tbsp. minced fresh cilantro
- 3   Tbsp. Thai chili sauce
- 2   Tbsp. sesame oil
- 2   tsp. minced garlic
- 1   lb. pork tenderloin, cut into ¼-in. slices
- ⅓   cup creamy peanut butter
- 3   Tbsp. hot water
- 2   tsp. lime juice

1. In a small bowl, combine the first 7 ingredients. Set aside ¼ cup for dipping sauce. Pour remaining sauce into a bowl or shallow dish; add the pork and turn to coat. Cover and refrigerate 30 minutes.

2. Drain pork, discarding marinade. Carefully thread the pork slices onto 20 metal or soaked wooden skewers. Place skewers in a greased 15x10x1-in. baking pan. Broil 3-4 in. from heat for roughly 3-4 minutes on each side or until meat juices run clear.

3. Meanwhile, for sauce, combine peanut butter and water in a small bowl until smooth. Stir in lime juice and reserved soy sauce mixture. Serve with skewers.

1 skewer: 73 cal., 4g fat (1g sat. fat), 13mg chol., 172mg sod., 4g carb. (2g sugars, 0 fiber), 6g pro. Diabetic exchanges: 1 lean meat, ½ fat.

PORK TENDERLOINS
WITH WILD RICE

||||||||||||||||||||||||||||||||||

The apricots say sweet things to the earthy herbs in this gravylicious meal. Remember this recipe—it's worthy of a weekend celebration.
—*Taste of Home* Test Kitchen

PREP: 25 MIN.
BAKE: 25 MIN. + STANDING
MAKES: 6 SERVINGS

- 2 pork tenderloins (1 lb. each)
- 1 pkg. (8.8 oz.) ready-to-serve whole grain brown and wild rice medley
- 1¾ cups frozen broccoli, carrots and water chestnuts, thawed and coarsely chopped
- ½ cup chopped dried apricots
- ½ cup minced fresh parsley
- ½ tsp. salt
- ½ tsp. garlic powder
- ½ tsp. dried thyme
- ½ tsp. dried sage leaves
- ¼ tsp. pepper

GRAVY
- 1 cup water
- 1 envelope pork gravy mix
- 1 Tbsp. Dijon mustard
- ¼ tsp. dried sage leaves
- 1 Tbsp. minced fresh parsley

1. Make a lengthwise slit down the center of each tenderloin to within ½ in. of bottom. Open tenderloins so they lie flat; cover and flatten to ¾-in. thickness.

2. Prepare rice according to package directions. In a small bowl, combine the rice, vegetables, apricots, parsley and seasonings.

3. Remove covering; spread rice mixture over meat. Close tenderloins; tie with kitchen string. Place in an ungreased 15x10x1-in. baking pan. Bake, uncovered, at 425° for 15 minutes.

4. Meanwhile, in a small saucepan, combine water, gravy mix, mustard and sage. Bring to a boil; cook and stir for 2 minutes or until thickened. Stir in parsley.

5. Brush 2 Tbsp. gravy over tenderloins. Bake 10-15 minutes longer or until a thermometer reads 160°. Let stand for 15 minutes. Discard the string; cut each tenderloin into 9 slices. Serve with remaining gravy.

|||||||||||||

3 slices with 2 Tbsp. gravy: 293 cal., 6g fat (2g sat. fat), 84mg chol., 803mg sod., 25g carb. (7g sugars, 2g fiber), 32g pro.

ZIPPY BREADED
PORK CHOPS

||||||||||||||||||||||||||||||||||||||

Need a perky update for pork chops? These chops with ranch dressing and a light breading will bring a delightful zing to your dinner table.
—Ann Ingalls, Gladstone, MO

TAKES: 25 MIN.
MAKES: 6 SERVINGS

- ⅓ **cup prepared ranch salad dressing**
- 1 **cup seasoned bread crumbs**
- 2 **Tbsp. grated Parmesan cheese**
- 6 **bone-in pork loin chops (8 oz. each)**

1. Preheat oven to 425°. Place salad dressing in a shallow bowl. In a separate shallow bowl, mix bread crumbs and cheese. Dip pork chops in dressing, then in crumb mixture, patting to help coating adhere.

2. Place on a rack in an ungreased 15x10x1-in. baking pan. Bake 15-20 minutes or until a thermometer reads 145°. Let stand 5 minutes before serving.

||||||||||||||

1 pork chop: 201 cal., 12g fat (3g sat. fat), 22mg chol., 437mg sod., 14g carb. (1g sugars, 1g fiber), 9g pro.

READER REVIEW
"These breaded baked pork chops were so tender and flavorful. I loved that they had a small ingredient list. Instead of dipping the chops in the ranch, I marinated them overnight in ranch dressing."
—BECKYJCARVER, TASTEOFHOME.COM

FISH & SEAFOOD MEALS

||||||||||||||||||||||

SHEET-PAN CHIPOTLE-LIME SHRIMP BAKE

I enjoy making this seafood dinner for company because it tastes amazing but takes very little effort to throw together. Use asparagus, Broccolini or a combination of the two. For me, it's all about what's available for a decent price.
—Colleen Delawder, Herndon, VA

PREP: 10 MIN.
BAKE: 40 MIN.
MAKES: 4 SERVINGS

- 1½ lbs. baby red potatoes, cut into ¾-in. cubes
- 1 Tbsp. extra virgin olive oil
- ¾ tsp. sea salt, divided
- 3 medium limes
- ¼ cup unsalted butter, melted
- 1 tsp. ground chipotle pepper
- ½ lb. fresh asparagus, trimmed
- ½ lb. Broccolini or broccoli, cut into small florets
- 1 lb. uncooked shrimp (16-20 per lb.), peeled and deveined
- 2 Tbsp. minced fresh cilantro

1. Preheat oven to 400°. Place potatoes in a greased 15x10x1-in. baking pan; drizzle with olive oil. Sprinkle with ¼ tsp. sea salt; stir to combine. Bake 30 minutes. Meanwhile, squeeze ⅓ cup juice from limes, reserving fruit. Combine lime juice, melted butter, chipotle and remaining sea salt.

2. Remove sheet pan from oven; stir the potatoes. Arrange asparagus, Broccolini, shrimp and reserved limes on top of potatoes. Pour lime juice mixture over vegetables and shrimp.

3. Bake until the shrimp turn pink and the vegetables are tender, about 10 minutes. Sprinkle with cilantro.

1 serving: 394 cal., 17g fat (8g sat. fat), 168mg chol., 535mg sod., 41g carb. (4g sugars, 6g fiber), 25g pro.

Follow the Recipe: *Don't throw out the squeezed limes. You'll be surprised by how much juice comes out of them after they're roasted, giving this dish even more citrus flavor.*

CHIMICHURRI
BAKED FLOUNDER

IIIIIIIIIIIIIIIIIIIIIIIIIIIIIIIIIIIIII

Chimichurri is a tasty uncooked sauce made from fresh herbs. I love it over any type of fish, but especially over baked flounder. To save time, I gather the herbs on my chopping board and chop them all at once.
—Jennifer Okutman, Westminster, MD

TAKES: 30 MIN.
MAKES: 4 SERVINGS

- 4 flounder or other lean white fish fillets (about 3 oz. each)
- ¼ tsp. garlic salt
- ½ cup olive oil
- 2 Tbsp. chopped fresh thyme
- 2 Tbsp. chopped fresh oregano
- 2 Tbsp. chopped fresh parsley
- 2 Tbsp. chopped fresh basil
- 2 Tbsp. chopped fresh chives
- 4 tsp. lemon juice
   Optional: Lemon wedges and additional herbs

Preheat oven to 350°. Place fillets in a 15x10x1-in. baking pan. Sprinkle with garlic salt. Bake until fish just begins to flake easily with a fork, 15-20 minutes. Meanwhile, whisk together oil, chopped herbs and lemon juice. Pour over cooked fillets. If desired, serve with lemon wedges and additional herbs.

IIIIIIIIIIIII

1 fillet with 3 Tbsp. sauce: 313 cal., 28g fat (4g sat. fat), 40mg chol., 186mg sod., 1g carb. (0 sugars, 0 fiber), 14g pro.

CAJUN PECAN
CATFISH

||||||||||||||||||||||||||||||||||||||

Instead of dredging the catfish to bread it, I just sprinkle the seasonings over the top. It's just as crunchy, but without the mess. Serve with biscuits and a side of mixed fruit.
—Jan Wilkins, Blytheville, AR

TAKES: 25 MIN.
MAKES: 4 SERVINGS

- 2   Tbsp. olive oil
- 2   tsp. lemon juice
- 1   tsp. Cajun seasoning
- ½   tsp. dried thyme
- ⅓   cup finely chopped pecans
- 2   Tbsp. grated Parmesan cheese
- 1   Tbsp. dry bread crumbs
- 1   Tbsp. dried parsley flakes
- 4   catfish fillets (6 oz. each)

1. Preheat oven to 425°. In a small bowl, combine oil, lemon juice, Cajun seasoning and thyme. In another bowl, combine pecans, cheese, bread crumbs, parsley and 1 Tbsp. of the oil mixture.

2. Place catfish in a greased 15x10x1-in. baking pan. Brush with remaining oil mixture. Spread pecan mixture over fillets. Bake until fish flakes easily with a fork, 10-15 minutes.

|||||||||||||

1 fillet: 377 cal., 28g fat (5g sat. fat), 82mg chol., 277mg sod., 3g carb. (1g sugars, 1g fiber), 29g pro.

FISH &
FRIES

IIIIIIIIIIIIIIIIIIIIIIIIIIIIIIIIIIIII

*Dine as though you're in a
traditional British pub. These
moist fish fillets from the oven
have a fuss-free coating that
is healthy but just as crispy
and golden as the deep-fried
kind. Simply seasoned, the
fresh-baked fries are perfect
on the side.*
—Janice Mitchell, Aurora, CO

PREP: 10 MIN.
BAKE: 35 MIN.
MAKES: 4 SERVINGS

- 1 **lb. potatoes
  (about 2 medium)**
- 2 **Tbsp. olive oil**
- ¼ **tsp. pepper**

FISH
- ⅓ **cup all-purpose flour**
- ¼ **tsp. pepper**
- 1 **large egg**
- 2 **Tbsp. water**
- ⅔ **cup crushed cornflakes**
- 1 **Tbsp. grated
  Parmesan cheese**
- ⅛ **tsp. cayenne pepper**
- 1 **lb. haddock or cod fillets
  Tartar sauce, optional**

1. Preheat oven to 425°. Peel and cut potatoes lengthwise into ½-in.-thick slices; cut slices into ½-in.-thick sticks.

2. In a large bowl, toss potatoes with oil and pepper. Transfer to a 15x10x1-in. baking pan coated with cooking spray. Bake, uncovered, 25-30 minutes or until golden brown and crisp, stirring once.

3. Meanwhile, in a shallow bowl, mix flour and pepper. In another shallow bowl, whisk egg with water. In a third bowl, toss cornflakes with cheese and cayenne. Dip fish in the flour mixture to coat both sides; shake off excess. Dip in the egg mixture, then in the cornflake mixture, patting to help coating adhere.

4. Place on a baking sheet coated with cooking spray. Bake 10-12 minutes or until fish just begins to flake easily with a fork. Serve with potatoes and, if desired, tartar sauce.

IIIIIIIIIIIII

*1 serving: 376 cal., 9g fat (2g sat. fat), 120mg chol.,
228mg sod., 44g carb. (3g sugars, 2g fiber), 28g pro.
Diabetic exchanges: 3 starch, 3 lean meat, 1½ fat.*

TILAPIA WITH
CORN SALSA

|||||||||||||||||||||||||||||||||||||

My family loves fish, and this super fast entree is popular at my house. Though it tastes as if it takes a long time, it cooks in minutes under the broiler. We like it garnished with lemon wedges and served with couscous on the side.
—Brenda Coffey, Singer Island, FL

TAKES: 10 MIN.
MAKES: 4 SERVINGS

- 4 tilapia fillets (6 oz. each)
- 1 Tbsp. olive oil
- ¼ tsp. salt
- ¼ tsp. pepper
- 1 can (15 oz.) black beans, rinsed and drained
- 1 can (11 oz.) whole kernel corn, drained
- ½ cup Italian salad dressing
- 2 Tbsp. chopped green onion
- 2 Tbsp. chopped sweet red pepper

1. Drizzle both sides of fillets with oil; sprinkle with salt and pepper.

2. Broil 4-6 in. from the heat until fish flakes easily with a fork, about 5-7 minutes. Meanwhile, in a small bowl, combine the remaining ingredients. Serve with the fish.

|||||||||||||

1 fillet with ¾ cup salsa: 354 cal., 10g fat (2g sat. fat), 83mg chol., 934mg sod., 25g carb. (7g sugars, 6g fiber), 38g pro.

ROSEMARY
SALMON & VEGGIES

||||||||||||||||||||||||||||||||||||||||

My husband and I eat a lot of salmon. One night while in a rush to get dinner on the table, I created this meal. It's a keeper! You can also include sliced zucchini, small cauliflower florets or fresh green beans.

—Elizabeth Bramkamp, Gig Harbor, WA

TAKES: 30 MIN.
MAKES: 4 SERVINGS

- 1½ lbs. salmon fillets, cut into 4 portions
- 2 Tbsp. melted coconut oil or olive oil
- 2 Tbsp. balsamic vinegar
- 2 tsp. minced fresh rosemary or ¾ tsp. dried rosemary, crushed
- 1 garlic clove, minced
- ½ tsp. salt
- 1 lb. fresh asparagus, trimmed
- 1 medium sweet red pepper, cut into 1-in. pieces
- ¼ tsp. pepper
  Lemon wedges

1. Preheat oven to 400°. Place salmon in a greased 15x10x1-in. baking pan. Combine the oil, vinegar, rosemary, garlic and salt. Pour half over salmon. Place asparagus and red pepper in a large bowl; drizzle with remaining oil mixture and toss to coat. Arrange around salmon in pan; sprinkle with pepper.

2. Bake until salmon flakes easily with a fork and vegetables are tender, 12-15 minutes. Serve with lemon wedges.

||||||||||||||

1 serving: 357 cal., 23g fat (9g sat. fat), 85mg chol., 388mg sod., 7g carb. (4g sugars, 2g fiber), 31g pro. Diabetic exchanges: 4 lean meat, 1½ fat, 1 vegetable.

TUNA
POTATO
SUPPER

IIIIIIIIIIIIIIIIIIIIIIIIIIIIIIIIIII

Tuna lovers will find this to be a real treat. My husband and I enjoy it as a nice change from the ordinary baked potato. Add a salad for a fast and simple lunch or dinner.
—Rosella Peters, Gull Lake, SK

TAKES: 25 MIN.
MAKES: 2 SERVINGS

 2   large baking potatoes
 1   can (6 oz.) light water-packed tuna, drained and flaked
 1   celery rib with leaves, finely chopped
 1   green onion, chopped
 ⅓   cup creamy cucumber salad dressing
 ⅛   tsp. each salt and pepper
 ¼   cup shredded Colby-Monterey Jack cheese

1. Scrub and pierce potatoes; place on a microwave-safe plate. Microwave, uncovered, on high until tender, turning once, 7-9 minutes. Cool slightly. Cut a thin slice off the top of each potato and discard. Scoop out the pulp, leaving a thin shell.

2. In a bowl, mash the pulp. Stir in the tuna, celery, onion, salad dressing, salt and pepper. Spoon into potato shells. Sprinkle with cheese. Place on a baking sheet. Broil 4-6 in. from the heat until cheese is melted, 5-6 minutes.

IIIIIIIIIIIII

1 potato: 598 cal., 25g fat (6g sat. fat), 38mg chol., 866mg sod., 63g carb. (0 sugars, 6g fiber), 30g pro.

READER REVIEW
"I loved this recipe. I think the next time I make it, I'm going to try adding corn to it. Very delicious."
—555444, TASTEOFHOME.COM

SPICY
SHRIMP-SLAW PITAS

||||||||||||||||||||||||||||||||||

My mother brought me peach salsa from Georgia, inspiring this recipe for shrimp pitas. Get awesome texture with edamame, or swap in some baby lima beans.
—Angela McClure, Cary, NC

PREP: 30 MIN.
BROIL: 5 MIN.
MAKES: 6 SERVINGS

1½ lbs. uncooked shrimp
    (31-40 per lb.),
    peeled, deveined and
    coarsely chopped
1 Tbsp. olive oil
1 tsp. paprika

SLAW
⅓ cup reduced-fat
    plain Greek yogurt
⅓ cup peach salsa or
    salsa of your choice
1 Tbsp. honey
½ tsp. salt
½ tsp. pepper
1 pkg. (12 oz.) broccoli
    coleslaw mix
2 cups fresh baby spinach
¼ cup shredded carrots
¼ cup frozen shelled
    edamame, thawed
12 whole wheat
    pita pocket halves

1. Preheat broiler. In a small bowl, toss shrimp with oil and paprika. Transfer to a foil-lined 15x10x1-in. baking pan. Broil 4-5 in. from heat until shrimp turn pink, stirring once, about 3-4 minutes.

2. In a small bowl, whisk yogurt, salsa, honey, salt and pepper. Add coleslaw mix, spinach, carrots, edamame and shrimp; toss to coat.

3. Place pita pockets on a baking sheet. Broil 4-5 in. from heat on each side or until lightly toasted, 1-2 minutes. Fill each pita half with ½ cup shrimp mixture.

|||||||||||||

2 filled pita halves: 322 cal., 6g fat (1g sat. fat), 139mg chol., 641mg sod., 41g carb. (7g sugars, 7g fiber), 28g pro. Diabetic exchanges: 3 lean meat, 2 starch, 1 vegetable, ½ fat.

DAD'S FAMOUS
STUFFIES

||||||||||||||||||||||||||||||||||||||

*The third of July is almost
as important as July Fourth
in my family. We make these
stuffies on the third every year,
and it's an event in and of itself!*
—Karen Barros, Bristol, RI

PREP: 1¼ HOURS
BAKE: 20 MIN.
MAKES: 10 SERVINGS

20 **fresh large quahog
    clams (about 10 lbs.)**
1 **lb. hot chourico or
    linguica (smoked
    Portuguese sausage)
    or fully cooked
    Spanish chorizo**
1 **large onion, chopped
    (about 2 cups)**
3 **tsp. seafood seasoning**
1 **pkg. (14 oz.) herb
    stuffing cubes**
1 **cup water
    Optional: Lemon wedges
    and hot pepper sauce**

1. Add 2 in. of water to a stockpot. Add clams and chourico; bring to a boil. Cover and steam 15-20 minutes or until the clams open.

2. Remove clams and sausage from pot, reserving 2 cups cooking liquid; cool slightly. Discard any unopened clams.

3. Preheat oven to 350°. Remove the clam meat from shells. Separate shells; reserve 30 half shells for stuffing. Place clam meat in a food processor; process until finely chopped. Transfer to a large bowl.

4. Remove the casings from sausage; cut sausage into 1½-in. pieces. Place in a food processor; process until finely chopped. Add sausage, onion and seafood seasoning to chopped clams. Stir in stuffing cubes. Add reserved cooking liquid and enough water to reach desired moistness, about 1 cup.

5. Spoon the clam mixture into reserved shells. Place in 15x10x1-in. baking pans. Bake until heated through, 15-20 minutes. Preheat broiler.

6. Broil the clams 4-6 in. from heat 4-5 minutes or until golden brown. If desired, serve with lemon wedges and pepper sauce.

FREEZE OPTION: Cover and freeze unbaked stuffed clams in a 15x10x1-in. baking pan until firm. Transfer to freezer containers; return to freezer. To use, place 3 stuffed clams on a microwave-safe plate. Cover with a paper towel; microwave on high until heated through, 3-4 minutes. Serve as directed.

||||||||||||||

3 stuffed clams: 296 cal., 11g fat (3g sat. fat), 71mg chol., 1188mg sod., 34g carb. (3g sugars, 2g fiber), 18g pro.

TUSCAN
FISH
PACKETS

||||||||||||||||||||||||||||||||||||

*My husband does a lot of
fishing, so I'm always looking
for different ways to serve his
catches. A professional chef
was kind enough to share this
recipe with me, and I played
around with some different
veggie combinations until I
found the one we liked best.*
—Kathy Morrow, Hubbard, OH

TAKES: 30 MIN.
MAKES: 4 SERVINGS

1   can (15 oz.) great
    northern beans,
    rinsed and drained
4   plum tomatoes, chopped
1   small zucchini, chopped
1   medium onion, chopped
1   garlic clove, minced
¼   cup white wine
¾   tsp. salt, divided
¼   tsp. pepper, divided
4   tilapia fillets (6 oz. each)
1   medium lemon,
    cut into 8 thin slices

1. Preheat oven to 400°. In a bowl, combine beans, tomatoes, zucchini, onion, garlic, wine, ½ tsp. salt and ⅛ tsp. pepper.

2. Rinse fish and pat dry. Place each fillet on an 18x12-in. piece of heavy-duty foil; season with the remaining salt and pepper. Spoon bean mixture over fish; top with lemon slices. Fold foil around fish and crimp edges to seal. Transfer packets to a baking sheet.

3. Bake until fish just begins to flake easily with a fork and vegetables are tender, 15-20 minutes. Be careful of escaping steam when opening packets.

|||||||||||||

*1 serving: 270 cal., 2g fat (1g sat. fat), 83mg chol.,
658mg sod., 23g carb. (4g sugars, 7g fiber), 38g pro.
Diabetic exchanges: 5 lean meat, 1 starch, 1 vegetable.*

__Be a Bean Queen:__ Great northern beans are small, tender white beans. Navy beans or cannellini beans are good substitutes.

AVOCADO
CRAB BOATS

IIIIIIIIIIIIIIIIIIIIIIIIIIIIII

*These boats are wonderful
with tortilla chips, beans or
rice. You can also cover them,
pack them on ice, and take
them to a picnic or a potluck.
Straight from the oven or cold,
they're always delicious.*
—Frances Benthin, Scio, OR

TAKES: 20 MIN.
MAKES: 8 SERVINGS

5 medium ripe avocados,
  peeled and halved
½ cup mayonnaise
2 Tbsp. lemon juice
2 cans (6 oz. each)
  lump crabmeat, drained
4 Tbsp. chopped
  fresh cilantro, divided
2 Tbsp. minced chives
1 serrano pepper,
  seeded and minced
1 Tbsp. capers, drained
¼ tsp. pepper
1 cup shredded
  pepper jack cheese
½ tsp. paprika
  Lemon wedges

1. Preheat broiler. Place 2 avocado halves in a large bowl; mash lightly with a fork. Add mayonnaise and lemon juice; mix until well blended. Stir in crab, 3 Tbsp. cilantro, chives, serrano pepper, capers and pepper. Spoon into remaining avocado halves.

2. Transfer to a 15x10x1-in. baking pan. Sprinkle with cheese and paprika. Broil 4-5 in. from heat until cheese is melted, about 3-5 minutes. Sprinkle with remaining cilantro; serve with lemon wedges.

IIIIIIIIIIII

1 filled avocado half: 325 cal., 28g fat (6g sat. fat), 57mg chol., 427mg sod., 8g carb. (0 sugars, 6g fiber), 13g pro.

HADDOCK
EN PAPILLOTE

||||||||||||||||||||||||||||||||||

This is a terrific dish for entertaining. It's easy to prepare, yet impressive. You can even assemble the bundles earlier in the day and then pop them in the oven 15 minutes before dinner.
—Amanda Singleton, Rogersville, TN

TAKES: 30 MIN.
MAKES: 4 SERVINGS

1½ lbs. haddock or
    cod fillet,
    cut into 4 portions
  4 Tbsp. dry white wine
  2 tsp. snipped fresh dill or
    1 tsp. dill weed
  1 tsp. grated lemon zest
  ½ cup julienned carrot
  ½ cup julienned zucchini
  4 Tbsp. slivered almonds,
    toasted
  4 Tbsp. butter

1. Preheat oven to 375°. Place each fillet portion on a piece of heavy-duty foil or parchment (about 12 in. square). Drizzle fillets with wine; sprinkle with dill and lemon zest. Top with the carrot, zucchini and almonds; dot with butter. Fold foil or parchment around fish, sealing tightly.

2. Place packets on a baking sheet. Bake until fish just begins to flake easily with a fork, 10-12 minutes. Open foil carefully to allow steam to escape.

||||||||||||||

1 packet: 311 cal., 16g fat (8g sat. fat), 129mg chol., 219mg sod., 4g carb. (2g sugars, 1g fiber), 34g pro.

Take It Outside: Looking for a knockout grilled supper? Toss the foil packets onto the grill for about 10 minutes.

COD &
ASPARAGUS BAKE

||||||||||||||||||||||||||||||||||||

The lemon pulls this flavorful and healthy dish together. You can also use grated Parmesan cheese instead of Romano.
—Thomas Faglon, Somerset, NJ

TAKES: 30 MIN.
MAKES: 4 SERVINGS

- 4 cod fillets (4 oz. each)
- 1 lb. fresh thin asparagus, trimmed
- 1 pint cherry tomatoes, halved
- 2 Tbsp. lemon juice
- 1½ tsp. grated lemon zest
- ¼ cup grated Romano cheese

1. Preheat oven to 375°. Place the cod and asparagus in a 15x10x1-in. baking pan brushed with oil. Add tomatoes, cut sides down. Brush fish with lemon juice; sprinkle with lemon zest. Sprinkle fish and vegetables with Romano cheese. Bake until the fish just begins to flake easily with a fork, about 12 minutes.

2. Remove pan from the oven; preheat broiler. Broil the cod mixture 3-4 in. from heat until vegetables are lightly browned, 2-3 minutes.

|||||||||||||

1 serving: 141 cal., 3g fat (2g sat. fat), 45mg chol., 184mg sod., 6g carb. (3g sugars, 2g fiber), 23g pro. Diabetic exchanges: 3 lean meat, 1 vegetable.

Times Are Changing: *We tested cod fillets that were about ¾ in. thick. You'll need to adjust the bake time up or down if your fillets are thicker or thinner.*

SHRIMP-STUFFED
POBLANO PEPPERS

IIIIIIIIIIIIIIIIIIIIIIIIIIIIIIIII

*Since my mom enjoys shrimp
and foods that are a bit on the
spicy side, I decided to create
shrimp-stuffed poblanos. She
was delighted with them!*
—Tina Garcia-Ortiz, Tampa, FL

PREP: 35 MIN.
BAKE: 10 MIN.
MAKES: 8 SERVINGS

- 4 **large poblano peppers**
- 2 **Tbsp. butter, melted, divided**
- 1 **tsp. coarsely ground pepper**
- ½ **tsp. kosher salt**
- 1 **small onion, finely chopped**
- 2 **celery ribs, chopped**
- 4 **oz. cream cheese, softened**
- 1 **lb. chopped cooked peeled shrimp**
- 1¾ **cups shredded Mexican cheese blend**
- 1½ **cups cooked rice**
- 2 **Tbsp. lemon juice**
- 2 **tsp. dried cilantro flakes**
- ½ **tsp. onion powder**
- ½ **tsp. garlic powder**

TOPPING
- 1 **cup panko bread crumbs**
- ¼ **cup grated Parmesan cheese**
- 2 **Tbsp. butter, melted**

1. Cut peppers in half lengthwise and discard seeds. Place peppers, cut side down, in an ungreased 15x10x1-in. baking pan. Brush with 1 Tbsp. butter; sprinkle with pepper and salt. Bake, uncovered, at 350° for 10-15 minutes or until tender.

2. Meanwhile, in a large skillet, saute onion and celery in remaining butter until tender. Stir in cream cheese until melted. Add the shrimp, cheese blend, rice, lemon juice and seasonings; heat through. Spoon into pepper halves.

3. Place in an ungreased 15x10x1-in. baking pan. Combine the topping ingredients; sprinkle over peppers. Bake, uncovered, at 350° for 10-15 minutes or until topping is golden brown.

IIIIIIIIIIIIII

1 stuffed pepper half: 361 cal., 21g fat (13g sat. fat), 153mg chol., 541mg sod., 20g carb. (2g sugars, 2g fiber), 23g pro.

SALMON WITH CREAMY DILL SAUCE

‖‖‖‖‖‖‖‖‖‖‖‖‖‖‖‖‖‖‖‖‖‖‖‖‖‖‖

There's nothing like fresh salmon, and my mom bakes it just right so it nearly melts in your mouth. The sour cream sauce is subtly seasoned with dill and horseradish so that it doesn't overpower the delicate salmon flavor.

—Susan Emery, Everett, WA

TAKES: 30 MIN.
MAKES: 6 SERVINGS

- 1 **salmon fillet (about 2 lbs.)**
- 1 **to 1½ tsp. lemon-pepper seasoning**
- 1 **tsp. onion salt**
- 1 **small onion, sliced and separated into rings**
- 6 **lemon slices**
- ¼ **cup butter, cubed**

DILL SAUCE

- ⅓ **cup sour cream**
- ⅓ **cup mayonnaise**
- 1 **Tbsp. finely chopped onion**
- 1 **tsp. lemon juice**
- 1 **tsp. prepared horseradish**
- ¾ **tsp. dill weed**
- ¼ **tsp. garlic salt**
  Pepper to taste

1. Line a 15x10x1-in. baking pan with heavy-duty foil; grease lightly. Place salmon skin side down on foil. Sprinkle with lemon pepper and onion salt. Top with the onion and lemon. Dot with butter. Fold foil around salmon; seal tightly,

2. Bake at 350° for 20 minutes. Open foil carefully, allowing steam to escape. Broil 4-6 in. from the heat for 3-5 minutes or until the fish flakes easily with a fork.

3. Meanwhile, combine the sauce ingredients until smooth. Serve with salmon.

‖‖‖‖‖‖‖‖‖‖‖

4 oz. cooked salmon with about 2 Tbsp. sauce: 418 cal., 33g fat (11g sat. fat), 100mg chol., 643mg sod., 3g carb. (1g sugars, 0 fiber), 26g pro.

Freezer-Friendly Fish: *You can freeze salmon and other oily types of fish, such as whitefish, mackerel and lake trout, for up to 3 months. Wrap fish in freezer paper, freezer bags or heavy-duty foil before freezing.*

SHEET-PAN TILAPIA &
VEGETABLE MEDLEY

IIIIIIIIIIIIIIIIIIIIIIIIIIIIIIIIIIIII

*Unlike some one-pan dinners
that require precooking in
a skillet or pot, this one uses
just the sheet pan.*
—Judy Batson, Tampa, FL

PREP: 15 MIN.
BAKE: 25 MIN.
MAKES: 2 SERVINGS

- 2 **medium
  Yukon Gold potatoes,
  cut into wedges**
- 3 **large fresh Brussels
  sprouts, thinly sliced**
- 3 **large radishes,
  thinly sliced**
- 1 **cup fresh
  sugar snap peas,
  cut into ½-in. pieces**
- 1 **small carrot,
  thinly sliced**
- 2 **Tbsp. butter, melted**
- ¼ **tsp. garlic salt**
- ½ **tsp. pepper**
- 2 **tilapia fillets (6 oz. each)**
- 2 **tsp. minced
  fresh tarragon or
  ½ tsp. dried tarragon**
- ⅛ **tsp. salt**
- 1 **Tbsp. butter, softened
  Optional: Lemon wedges
  and tartar sauce**

1. Preheat oven to 450°. Line a 15x10x1-in. baking pan with foil; grease foil.

2. In a large bowl, combine the first 5 ingredients. Add melted butter, garlic salt and pepper; toss to coat. Place vegetables in a single layer in prepared pan; bake until potatoes are tender, about 20 minutes.

3. Remove from oven; preheat broiler. Arrange vegetables on 1 side of sheet pan. Add fish to other side. Sprinkle fillets with tarragon and salt; dot with softened butter. Broil 4-5 in. from heat until fish flakes easily with a fork, about 5 minutes. If desired, serve with lemon wedges and tartar sauce.

IIIIIIIIIIIII

1 serving: 555 cal., 20g fat (12g sat. fat), 129mg chol., 892mg sod., 56g carb. (8g sugars, 8g fiber), 41g pro.

Mellow Out: *A quick roast softens radishes nicely
and helps mellow out the sharp flavor that some
older radishes may have.*

MEATLESS
STAPLES
||||||||||||||||||||

TOMATO
BAGUETTE
PIZZA

IIIIIIIIIIIIIIIIIIIIIIIIIIIIIIIIIIIIIII

When my tomatoes ripen all at once, I use them up in simple recipes. These cheesy baguette pizzas, served with a salad, are ideal for lunch—and they make standout appetizers, too.
—LORRAINE CALAND, SHUNIAH, ON

PREP: 25 MIN.
BAKE: 10 MIN.
MAKES: 6 SERVINGS

- 2 tsp. olive oil
- 8 oz. sliced fresh mushrooms
- 2 medium onions, halved and sliced
- 2 garlic cloves, minced
- ½ tsp. Italian seasoning
- ¼ tsp. salt
  Dash pepper
- 1 French bread baguette (10½ oz.), halved lengthwise
- 1½ cups shredded part-skim mozzarella cheese
- ¾ cup thinly sliced fresh basil leaves, divided
- 3 medium tomatoes, sliced

1. Preheat oven to 400°. In a large skillet, heat olive oil over medium-high heat; saute mushrooms and onions until tender. Add garlic and seasonings; cook and stir 1 minute.

2. Place baguette halves on a baking sheet, cut side up; sprinkle with half the mozzarella cheese and ½ cup basil. Top with the mushroom mixture, tomatoes and remaining cheese.

3. Bake until cheese is melted, 10-15 minutes. Sprinkle with remaining basil. Cut each half into 3 portions.

IIIIIIIIIIIII

1 piece: 260 cal., 7g fat (4g sat. fat), 18mg chol., 614mg sod., 36g carb. (5g sugars, 3g fiber), 13g pro. Diabetic exchanges: 2 starch, 1 vegetable, 1 medium-fat meat.

READER REVIEW
"This was, by far, the best pizza we've ever eaten. The texture of the baguette was crisp on the outside and chewy once you bit in to it. Absolutely the best!"
—ANNECOOKS, TASTEOFHOME.COM

GARDEN
VEGETABLE
GNOCCHI

||||||||||||||||||||||||||||||||||

When we go meatless at our house, we toss gnocchi (my husband's favorite) with a few veggies and a dab of prepared pesto. I use zucchini in this 30-minute dish, too.
—Elisabeth Larsen, Pleasant Grove, UT

TAKES: 30 MIN.
MAKES: 4 SERVINGS

- 2 medium yellow summer squash, sliced
- 1 medium sweet red pepper, chopped
- 8 oz. sliced fresh mushrooms
- 1 Tbsp. olive oil
- ¼ tsp. salt
- ¼ tsp. pepper
- 1 pkg. (16 oz.) potato gnocchi
- ½ cup Alfredo sauce
- ¼ cup prepared pesto
      Chopped fresh basil, optional

1. Preheat oven to 450°. In a greased 15x10x1-in. baking pan, toss vegetables with oil, salt and pepper. Roast 18-22 minutes or until tender, stirring once.

2. Meanwhile, in a large saucepan, cook gnocchi according to package directions. Drain and return to pan.

3. Stir in the roasted vegetables, Alfredo sauce and pesto. If desired, sprinkle with basil.

|||||||||||||

1½ cups: 402 cal., 14g fat (4g sat. fat), 17mg chol., 955mg sod., 57g carb. (12g sugars, 5g fiber), 13g pro.

BLACK BEAN CAKES WITH
MOLE SALSA

||||||||||||||||||||||||||||||||

Homemade salsa adds zip to this mouthwatering meatless entree. Serve the patties on a bun for scrumptious veggie burgers your family will love.
—Roxanne Chan, Albany, CA

TAKES: 30 MIN.
MAKES: 6 SERVINGS
(1¼ CUPS SALSA)

- 1 can (15 oz.) black beans, rinsed and drained
- 1 large egg, beaten
- 1 cup shredded zucchini
- ½ cup dry bread crumbs
- ¼ cup shredded Mexican cheese blend
- 2 Tbsp. chili powder
- ¼ tsp. salt
- ¼ tsp. baking powder
- ¼ tsp. ground cumin
- 2 Tbsp. olive oil

SALSA
- 2 medium tomatoes, chopped
- 1 small green pepper, chopped
- 3 Tbsp. grated chocolate
- 1 green onion, thinly sliced
- 2 Tbsp. minced fresh cilantro
- 1 Tbsp. lime juice
- 1 to 2 tsp. minced chipotle pepper in adobo sauce
- 1 tsp. honey

1. In a small bowl, mash beans. Add the egg, zucchini, bread crumbs, cheese, chili powder, salt, baking powder and cumin; mix well.

2. Shape into 6 patties; brush both sides with olive oil. Place on a baking sheet.

3. Broil 3-4 in. from the heat for 3-4 minutes on each side or until a thermometer reads 160°.

4. Meanwhile, in a small bowl, combine the salsa ingredients. Serve with black bean cakes.

|||||||||||||

1 cake with 3 Tbsp. salsa: 206 cal., 10g fat (3g sat. fat), 39mg chol., 397mg sod., 23g carb. (4g sugars, 6g fiber), 8g pro. Diabetic exchanges: 2 fat, 1½ starch, 1 lean meat.

VEGGIE PIZZA

||||||||||||||||||||||||||||||||||||

When I was thinking about what my family likes to eat and what I like to cook, the answer was simple—pizza!
—Dana Dirks, San Diego, CA

PREP: 30 MIN. + STANDING
BAKE: 10 MIN.
MAKES: 6 SERVINGS

- 1 pkg. (¼ oz.) active dry yeast
- 1 cup warm water (110° to 115°)
- ⅓ cup grated Parmesan cheese
- 2 Tbsp. canola oil
- 1 Tbsp. sugar
- 1 Tbsp. dried basil
- ½ tsp. salt
- ¾ cup all-purpose flour
- 1 to 1½ cups whole wheat flour
- 3½ cups fresh baby spinach
- ¼ cup prepared pesto
- 1¾ cups coarsely chopped fresh broccoli
- ¾ cup chopped green pepper
- 2 green onions, chopped
- 4 garlic cloves, minced
- 2 cups shredded part-skim mozzarella cheese

1. In a small bowl, dissolve yeast in warm water. Add the Parmesan cheese, oil, sugar, basil, salt, all-purpose flour and ¾ cup whole wheat flour. Beat until smooth. Stir in enough remaining whole wheat flour to form a soft dough (dough will be sticky).

2. Turn onto a lightly floured surface; knead until smooth and elastic, 6-8 minutes. Cover and let rest for 10 minutes.

3. Roll dough into a 16x12-in. rectangle. Transfer to a baking sheet coated with cooking spray; build up edges slightly. Prick the dough with a fork. Bake at 375° until lightly browned, 8-10 minutes.

4. Meanwhile, in a large saucepan, bring ½ in. of water to a boil. Add the spinach; cover and boil until wilted, 3-5 minutes. Drain and place in a food processor. Add pesto; cover and process until blended.

5. Spread over pizza crust. Top with broccoli, green pepper, green onions, garlic and mozzarella cheese. Bake until cheese is melted, 10-12 minutes.

|||||||||||||

1 piece: 364 cal., 17g fat (6g sat. fat), 29mg chol., 543mg sod., 35g carb. (5g sugars, 5g fiber), 19g pro. Diabetic exchanges: 2 starch, 2 medium-fat meat, 2 fat, 1 vegetable.

ROASTED
BUTTERNUT SQUASH TACOS

||||||||||||||||||||||||||||||||||

Spicy butternut squash makes the base for these vegetarian tacos. I'm always looking for easy and nutritious weeknight dinners for my family, and these are a delicious solution.
—Elisabeth Larsen, Pleasant Grove, UT

PREP: 10 MIN.
BAKE: 30 MIN.
MAKES: 6 SERVINGS

- 2 Tbsp. canola oil
- 1 Tbsp. chili powder
- ½ tsp. ground cumin
- ½ tsp. ground coriander
- ½ tsp. salt
- ¼ tsp. cayenne pepper
- 1 medium butternut squash (3 to 4 lbs.), peeled and cut into ½-in. pieces
- 12 corn tortillas (6 in.), warmed
- 1 cup crumbled queso fresco or feta cheese
- 1 medium ripe avocado, peeled and sliced thin
- ¼ cup diced red onion
  Pico de gallo, optional

1. Preheat oven to 425°. Combine first 6 ingredients. Add squash cubes; toss to coat. Transfer to a foil-lined 15x10x1-in. baking pan. Bake squash, stirring occasionally, until tender, 30-35 minutes.

2. Divide squash evenly among tortillas. Top with queso fresco, avocado and red onion. If desired, serve with pico de gallo.

||||||||||||

2 tacos: 353 cal., 13g fat (3g sat. fat), 13mg chol., 322mg sod., 54g carb. (7g sugars, 13g fiber), 11g pro.

NO-FRY
BLACK BEAN CHIMICHANGAS

||||||||||||||||||||||||||||||||||

*My chimichangas get lovin'
from the oven so they're a bit
healthier. Black beans provide
protein, and it's a smart way to
use up leftover rice.*
—Kimberly Hammond, Kingwood, TX

TAKES: 25 MIN.
MAKES: 6 SERVINGS

- 2 **cans (15 oz. each) black beans, rinsed and drained**
- 1 **pkg. (8.8 oz.) ready-to-serve brown rice**
- ⅔ **cup frozen corn**
- ⅔ **cup minced fresh cilantro**
- ⅔ **cup chopped green onions**
- ½ **tsp. salt**
- 6 **whole wheat tortillas (8 in.), warmed if necessary**
- 4 **tsp. olive oil, divided Guacamole and salsa, optional**

1. Preheat broiler. In a large microwave-safe bowl, mix beans, rice and corn; microwave, covered, until mixture is heated through, 4-5 minutes, stirring halfway. Stir in cilantro, green onions and salt.

2. To assemble, spoon ¾ cup bean mixture across the center of each tortilla. Fold bottom and sides of tortilla over filling and roll up. Place on a greased baking sheet, seam side down.

3. Brush tops with 2 tsp. oil. Broil 3-4 in. from the heat until golden brown, 45-60 seconds. Turn over; brush tops with remaining oil. Broil until golden brown, 45-60 seconds longer. If desired, serve with guacamole and salsa.

||||||||||||

1 chimichanga: 337 cal., 5g fat (0 sat. fat), 0 chol., 602mg sod., 58g carb. (2g sugars, 10g fiber), 13g pro.

Make Them Meaty: You can make these chimichangas for meat lovers, too. Just follow the cooking method while experimenting with fillings such as cooked chicken, ground beef or shredded pork.

BROILED CHEESE
STUFFED
PORTOBELLOS

||||||||||||||||||||||||||||||||||||

My vegetarian friends do the happy dance for my marinated mushroom caps featuring a filling of spinach, cream cheese, mozzarella and Parmesan. As a twist, use button mushrooms and make appetizers instead.
—Jennifer Bender, Baldwin, GA

TAKES: 30 MIN.
MAKES: 6 SERVINGS

- 6 large portobello mushrooms (4 to 4½ in.), stems removed
- ⅔ cup Italian salad dressing
- 1 pkg. (10 oz.) frozen chopped spinach, thawed and squeezed dry
- 1 pkg. (8 oz.) cream cheese, softened
- ¼ cup grated Parmesan cheese
- 3 garlic cloves, minced
- ⅛ tsp. salt
- ⅛ tsp. pepper
- 6 slices part-skim mozzarella cheese

1. Preheat broiler. In a large bowl, combine mushrooms and salad dressing and turn to coat. Let stand 15 minutes. Meanwhile, in another large bowl, combine spinach, cream cheese, Parmesan cheese, garlic, salt and pepper.

2. Drain the mushrooms, discarding salad dressing. Place mushrooms in a foil-lined 15x10x1-in. baking pan. Broil 3-4 in. from heat 2-3 minutes on each side or until tender. Fill with spinach mixture; top with mozzarella cheese. Broil 2-4 minutes longer or until cheese is melted.

|||||||||||||||

1 stuffed mushroom: 314 cal., 24g fat (11g sat. fat), 63mg chol., 710mg sod., 13g carb. (5g sugars, 3g fiber), 14g pro.

CHEESY
SUMMER SQUASH
FLATBREADS

IIIIIIIIIIIIIIIIIIIIIIIIIIIIIIII

*When you want a meatless
meal with Mediterranean style,
these flatbreads smothered
with squash, hummus and
mozzarella deliver the goods.*
—Matthew Hass, Ellison Bay, WI

TAKES: 30 MIN.
MAKES: 4 SERVINGS

 3   small yellow summer
     squash, sliced ¼ in.
     thick
 1   Tbsp. olive oil
 ½   tsp. salt
 2   cups fresh baby spinach,
     coarsely chopped
 2   naan flatbreads
 ⅓   cup roasted red pepper
     hummus
 1   carton (8 oz.) fresh
     mozzarella cheese
     pearls
     Pepper

1. Preheat oven to 425°. Toss squash with olive oil and salt;
spread evenly in a 15x10x1-in. baking pan. Roast until tender,
8-10 minutes. Transfer to a bowl; stir in spinach.

2. Place naan on a baking sheet; spread with hummus. Top with
squash mixture and mozzarella. Bake on a lower oven rack just
until cheese is melted, 4-6 minutes. Sprinkle with pepper.

IIIIIIIIIIIIII

*½ topped flatbread: 332 cal., 20g fat (9g sat. fat), 47mg
chol., 737mg sod., 24g carb. (7g sugars, 3g fiber), 15g pro.*

ROASTED CURRIED
CHICKPEAS
& CAULIFLOWER

IIIIIIIIIIIIIIIIIIIIIIIIIIIIIIIIII

When there's not much time to cook, try roasting potatoes and cauliflower with chickpeas for a warm-you-up dinner. Add tofu or cooked chicken to the sheet pan if you like.
—Pam Correll, Brockport, PA

PREP: 15 MIN.
BAKE: 30 MIN.
MAKES: 4 SERVINGS

2   lbs. potatoes (about 4 medium), peeled and cut into ½-in. cubes
1   small head cauliflower, broken into florets (about 3 cups)
1   can (15 oz.) chickpeas or garbanzo beans, rinsed and drained
3   Tbsp. olive oil
2   tsp. curry powder
¾   tsp. salt
¼   tsp. pepper
3   Tbsp. minced fresh cilantro or parsley

1. Preheat oven to 400°. Place first 7 ingredients in a large bowl; toss to coat. Transfer to a 15x10x1-in. baking pan coated with cooking spray.

2. Roast until vegetables are tender, 30-35 minutes, stirring occasionally. Sprinkle with cilantro.

IIIIIIIIIIIII

1½ cups: 339 cal., 13g fat (2g sat. fat), 0 chol., 605mg sod., 51g carb. (6g sugars, 8g fiber), 8g pro. Diabetic exchanges: 3 starch, 2 fat, 1 vegetable, 1 lean meat.

READER REVIEW
"Great simple vegetarian weeknight dinner! I also like it with a little squeeze of lime juice at the end."
—CURLYLIS85, TASTEOFHOME.COM

APPLE, WHITE CHEDDAR
& ARUGULA TARTS

|||||||||||||||||||||||||||||||||||

These tarts remind me of fall in Michigan, where I grew up. Add meat if you like or keep things light. I always like to garnish them with fried prosciutto.
—Maria Davis, Hermosa Beach, CA

TAKES: 30 MIN.
MAKES: 4 SERVINGS

- 1 **sheet frozen puff pastry, thawed**
- 1 **cup shredded white cheddar cheese**
- 2 **medium apples, thinly sliced**
- 2 **Tbsp. olive oil**
- 1 **Tbsp. lemon juice**
- 3 **cups fresh arugula or baby spinach**

1. Preheat oven to 400°. On a lightly floured surface, unfold puff pastry; roll into a 12-in. square. Cut pastry into 4 squares; place on a parchment-lined baking sheet.

2. Sprinkle half of each square with cheese to within ¼ in. of edges; top with apples. Fold pastry over filling. Press edges with a fork to seal. Bake until golden brown, 16-18 minutes.

3. In a bowl, whisk olive oil and lemon juice until blended; add arugula and toss to coat. Serve with tarts.

|||||||||||||

1 tart: 518 cal., 33g fat (10g sat. fat), 29mg chol., 389mg sod., 46g carb. (8g sugars, 7g fiber), 12g pro.

EGGPLANT FLATBREAD PIZZAS

|||||||||||||||||||||||||||||||||||||||||

I loved to make these back in my home cooking days. Now I'm a chef!
—Christine Wendland, Browns Mills, NJ

TAKES: 30 MIN.
MAKES: 4 SERVINGS

- 3 Tbsp. olive oil, divided
- 2½ cups cubed eggplant (½ in.)
- 1 small onion, halved and thinly sliced
- ½ tsp. salt
- ⅛ tsp. pepper
- 1 garlic clove, minced
- 2 naan flatbreads
- ½ cup part-skim ricotta cheese
- 1 tsp. dried oregano
- ½ cup roasted garlic tomato sauce
- ½ cup loosely packed basil leaves
- 1 cup shredded part-skim mozzarella cheese
- 2 Tbsp. grated Parmesan cheese
  Sliced fresh basil, optional

1. Preheat oven to 400°. In a large skillet, heat 1 Tbsp. oil over medium-high heat; saute eggplant and onion with salt and pepper until eggplant begins to soften, 4-5 minutes. Stir in garlic; remove from heat.

2. Place naan on a baking sheet. Spread with ricotta cheese; sprinkle with oregano. Spread with tomato sauce. Top with the eggplant mixture and whole basil leaves. Sprinkle with mozzarella and Parmesan cheeses; drizzle with remaining oil.

3. Bake until crust is golden brown and the cheese is melted, 12-15 minutes. If desired, top with sliced basil.

||||||||||||

½ pizza: 340 cal., 21g fat (7g sat. fat), 32mg chol., 996mg sod., 25g carb. (5g sugars, 3g fiber), 14g pro.

Simple Substitution: *Roasted garlic tomato sauce may be replaced with any flavored tomato sauce or a meatless pasta sauce.*

BLACK BEAN
TORTILLA PIE

||||||||||||||||||||||||||||||||||||

I found this entree a while ago but decreased the cheese and increased the herbs originally called for by a bit. It's one of my toddler's favorite meals. She always smiles when she sees it on the table.
—Wendy Kelly, Petersburg, NY

PREP: 50 MIN.
BAKE: 15 MIN.
MAKES: 6 SERVINGS

- 1 Tbsp. olive oil
- 1 medium green pepper, chopped
- 1 medium onion, chopped
- 1 tsp. ground cumin
- ¼ tsp. pepper
- 3 garlic cloves, minced
- 2 cans (15 oz. each) black beans, rinsed and drained
- 1 can (14½ oz.) vegetable broth
- 1 pkg. (10 oz.) frozen corn, thawed
- 4 green onions, sliced
- 4 flour tortillas (8 in.)
- 1 cup shredded reduced-fat cheddar cheese, divided

1. Preheat oven to 400°. In a large skillet, heat oil over medium-high heat. Add green pepper, onion, cumin and pepper; cook and stir until vegetables are tender. Add the garlic; cook 1 minute longer.

2. Stir in beans and broth. Bring to a boil; cook until liquid is reduced to about ⅓ cup, stirring occasionally. Stir in corn and green onions; remove from heat.

3. Place 1 tortilla in a 9-in. springform pan coated with cooking spray. Layer with 1½ cups of the bean mixture and ¼ cup of cheese. Repeat layers twice. Top with the remaining tortilla. Place pan on a baking sheet.

4. Bake, uncovered, until pie is heated through, 15-20 minutes. Sprinkle with remaining cheese. Loosen sides from pan with a knife; remove rim from pan. Cut into 6 wedges.

||||||||||||||

1 slice: 353 cal., 9g fat (3g sat. fat), 14mg chol., 842mg sod., 53g carb. (6g sugars, 8g fiber), 17g pro. Diabetic exchanges: 3 starch, 1 lean meat, 1 very lean meat, 1 vegetable, 1 fat.

PORTOBELLO & CHICKPEA
SHEET-PAN SUPPER

||||||||||||||||||||||||||||||||

This is a fantastic meatless dinner as well as an amazing side dish. It works well with a variety of sheet-pan-roasted vegetables. We enjoy using zucchini or yellow squash in the summer. You can also change up the herbs you use in the dressing.
—Elisabeth Larsen, Pleasant Grove, UT

PREP: 15 MIN.
BAKE: 35 MIN.
MAKES: 4 SERVINGS

- ¼ cup olive oil
- 2 Tbsp. balsamic vinegar
- 1 Tbsp. minced fresh oregano
- ¾ tsp. garlic powder
- ½ tsp. salt
- ¼ tsp. pepper
- 1 can (15 oz.) chickpeas or garbanzo beans, rinsed and drained
- 4 large portobello mushrooms (4 to 4½ in.), stems removed
- 1 lb. fresh asparagus, trimmed and cut into 2-in. pieces
- 8 oz. cherry tomatoes

1. Preheat oven to 400°. In a small bowl, combine the first 6 ingredients. Toss the chickpeas with 2 Tbsp. oil mixture. Transfer to a 15x10x1-in. baking pan. Bake 20 minutes.

2. Brush the mushrooms with 1 Tbsp. oil mixture; add to pan. Toss asparagus and tomatoes with remaining oil mixture; arrange around mushrooms. Bake until vegetables are tender, 15-20 minutes longer.

||||||||||||

1 mushroom with 1 cup vegetables: 279 cal., 16g fat (2g sat. fat), 0 chol., 448mg sod., 28g carb. (8g sugars, 7g fiber), 8g pro. Diabetic exchanges: 3 fat, 2 starch.

SPINACH FETA
TURNOVERS

IIIIIIIIIIIIIIIIIIIIIIIIIIIIIIIIII

These quick turnovers, one of my wife's favorites, are so easy to make with pizza crust. They're melt-in-your-mouth comfort food.
—David Baruch, Weston, FL

TAKES: 30 MIN.
MAKES: 4 SERVINGS

- 2   **large eggs**
- 1   **pkg. (10 oz.) frozen leaf spinach, thawed, squeezed dry and chopped**
- ¾   **cup crumbled feta cheese**
- 2   **garlic cloves, minced**
- ¼   **tsp. pepper**
- 1   **tube (13.8 oz.) refrigerated pizza crust Refrigerated tzatziki sauce, optional**

1. In a bowl, whisk eggs; set aside 1 Tbsp. of eggs. Combine the spinach, feta cheese, garlic, pepper and the remaining beaten eggs.

2. Unroll pizza crust; roll into a 12-in. square. Cut into four 6-in. squares. Top each square with about ⅓ cup spinach mixture. Fold into a triangle and pinch edges to seal. Cut slits in top; brush with reserved egg.

3. Place on a greased baking sheet. Bake at 425° until golden brown, 10-12 minutes. If desired, serve with tzatziki sauce.

IIIIIIIIIIII

1 turnover: 361 cal., 9g fat (4g sat. fat), 104mg chol., 936mg sod., 51g carb. (7g sugars, 4g fiber), 17g pro.

MOZZARELLA
CORNBREAD
PIZZA

IIIIIIIIIIIIIIIIIIIIIIIIIIIIIIIIIIIIII

*My sons like pizza but not
takeout, so I pull out my trusty
baking pan to make cornbread
pizza with veggies in the crust.
Adjust the toppings as you like.*
—Mary Leverette, Columbia, SC

PREP: 25 MIN. + STANDING
BAKE: 20 MIN.
MAKES: 10 SERVINGS

3 **cups shredded zucchini**
1 **tsp. salt, divided**
2 **pkg. (8½ oz. each)
   vegetarian cornbread/
   muffin mix**
3 **large eggs, lightly
   beaten**
¼ **tsp. pepper**

TOPPINGS
1 **jar (14 oz.) pizza sauce**
¾ **cup chopped sweet red
   or green pepper**
1 **can (2¼ oz.) sliced ripe
   olives, drained**
4 **green onions, chopped**
⅓ **cup coarsely chopped
   fresh basil**
1 **Tbsp. minced fresh
   oregano or 1 tsp. dried
   oregano**
3 **cups shredded
   part-skim mozzarella
   cheese**

1. Preheat oven to 450°. Place zucchini in a colander over a
bowl; sprinkle with ¾ tsp. salt and toss. Let stand 15 minutes.

2. Press zucchini and blot dry with paper towels; transfer to a
large bowl. Add cornbread mixes, eggs, pepper and remaining
salt; stir until blended. Spread evenly into a greased 15x10x1-in.
baking pan. Bake until lightly browned, 8-10 minutes. Reduce
oven setting to 350°.

3. Spread pizza sauce over crust. Top with red pepper, olives
and green onions. Sprinkle with herbs and cheese. Bake until
cheese is melted, 12-15 minutes.

IIIIIIIIIIIII

*1 piece: 366 cal., 15g fat (6g sat. fat), 79mg chol., 912mg
sod., 42g carb. (14g sugars, 5g fiber), 15g pro.*

BALSAMIC ROASTED
VEGETABLE PRIMAVERA

||||||||||||||||||||||||||||||||||||

Roasting makes these end-of-summer veggies irresistible. Toss them with balsamic and pasta for a light but filling dinner.
—Carly Curtin, Ellicott City, MD

PREP: 15 MIN.
BAKE: 20 MIN.
MAKES: 4 SERVINGS

- 4 medium carrots, sliced
- 2 medium zucchini, coarsely chopped (about 3 cups)
- 1⅔ cups cherry tomatoes
- ¼ cup olive oil
- 3 Tbsp. balsamic vinegar
- 1 Tbsp. minced fresh thyme or 1 tsp. dried thyme
- 2 tsp. minced fresh rosemary or ½ tsp. dried rosemary, crushed
- 1 tsp. salt
- ½ tsp. garlic powder
- 8 oz. uncooked rigatoni or whole wheat rigatoni
- ¼ cup shredded Parmesan cheese

1. Preheat oven to 400°. Combine carrots, zucchini and tomatoes in a greased 15x10x1-in. baking pan. Whisk together next 6 ingredients; reserve half. Drizzle remaining balsamic mixture over vegetables; toss to coat. Bake until carrots are crisp-tender, 20-25 minutes.

2. Meanwhile, cook rigatoni according to package directions; drain. Toss rigatoni with roasted vegetables, pan juices and reserved balsamic mixture. Sprinkle with cheese.

|||||||||||||

1½ cups: 410 cal., 17g fat (3g sat. fat), 4mg chol., 731mg sod., 56g carb. (12g sugars, 5g fiber), 12g pro.

Summer's Bounty: *If your garden is overflowing with large tomatoes, swap 2 in place of the cherry tomatoes. Similarly, if you have extra fresh herbs on hand, don't be afraid to sprinkle some on just before serving. You'll be amazed at how they perk up a dish.*

DESSERT
FROM THE
SHEET PAN
||||||||||||||||||||

BANANA SPLIT
CAKE BARS

||||||||||||||||||||||||||||||||||||||||||

*Summer isn't summer without
a banana split or two. These
fun bars bring that same
delicious flavor in potluck-
perfect form.*
—Jasey McBurnett, Rock Springs, WY

PREP: 25 MIN.
BAKE: 25 MIN. + COOLING
MAKES: 2 DOZEN

- ½ cup butter, softened
- 1½ cups sugar
- 2 large eggs,
  room temperature
- 1½ cups mashed ripe
  bananas (about 3 large)
- 1 cup sour cream
- 2 tsp. vanilla extract
- 2 cups all-purpose flour
- 1 tsp. baking soda
- ¾ tsp. salt
- 2 jars (10 oz. each)
  maraschino cherries,
  drained and chopped
- 2 cups semisweet
  chocolate chips
- 1 pkg. (10 oz.) miniature
  marshmallows
  Optional: Chopped
  salted peanuts and
  banana slices or
  dried banana chips

1. Preheat oven to 375°. Grease a 15x10x1-in. baking pan.

2. In a large bowl, beat butter and sugar until crumbly, about 2 minutes. Add eggs; mix well. Beat in bananas, sour cream and vanilla. In another bowl, whisk flour, baking soda and salt; gradually add to butter mixture. Transfer to prepared pan.

3. Bake until a toothpick inserted in center comes out clean, 18-20 minutes. Top the cake with cherries, chocolate chips, marshmallows and, if desired, peanuts. Bake until chips are slightly melted and marshmallows puff, 3-5 minutes longer. Cool completely in pan on a wire rack; cut into bars. If desired, top with banana slices or banana chips before serving.

|||||||||||||

*1 piece: 294 cal., 11g fat (6g sat. fat), 28mg chol.,
177mg sod., 52g carb. (38g sugars, 1g fiber), 3g pro.*

*Grab a Fork and Dig In: These bars are loaded with
amazing toppings, making them a bit tricky to cut into
hand-held bars. Plan to eat them with a fork to scoop
up all the goodies that fall off.*

PUMPKIN
CAKE
ROLL

IIIIIIIIIIIIIIIIIIIIIIIIIIIIIIIIIIIIIIII

This lovely cake is a slice of heaven—especially if you like cream cheese and pumpkin. With such excellent attributes, it is worth considering as a fancy alternative to pumpkin pie for Thanksgiving dessert.
—Elizabeth Montgomery, Allston, MA

PREP: 25 MIN.
BAKE: 15 MIN. + CHILLING
MAKES: 10 SERVINGS

- 3 **large eggs,**
  room temperature
- 1 **cup sugar**
- ⅔ **cup canned pumpkin**
- 1 **tsp. lemon juice**
- ¾ **cup all-purpose flour**
- 2 **tsp. ground cinnamon**
- 1 **tsp. baking powder**
- ½ **tsp. salt**
- ¼ **tsp. ground nutmeg**
- 1 **cup finely chopped**
  walnuts

CREAM CHEESE FILLING
- 6 **oz. cream cheese,**
  softened
- 1 **cup confectioners' sugar**
- ¼ **cup butter, softened**
- ½ **tsp. vanilla extract**
  Additional
  confectioners' sugar

1. In a large bowl, beat eggs on high for 5 minutes. Gradually beat in sugar until thick and lemon-colored. Add pumpkin and lemon juice. Combine the flour, cinnamon, baking powder, salt and nutmeg; fold into the pumpkin mixture.

2. Grease a 15x10x1-in. baking pan and line with parchment. Grease and flour the paper. Spread batter into pan; sprinkle with walnuts. Bake at 375° for 15 minutes or until the cake springs back when lightly touched.

3. Immediately turn out onto a clean dish towel dusted with confectioners' sugar. Peel off paper and roll cake up in towel, starting with a short end. Cool.

4. Meanwhile, in a large bowl, beat the cream cheese, sugar, butter and vanilla until fluffy. Carefully unroll the cake. Spread filling over cake to within 1 in. of edges. Roll up again. Cover and chill until serving. Dust with confectioners' sugar.

IIIIIIIIIIIII

1 slice: 365 cal., 20g fat (8g sat. fat), 85mg chol., 279mg sod., 44g carb. (33g sugars, 2g fiber), 6g pro.

> *Keep It Level: Want to make sure a sheet-pan cake bakes evenly? Start by using a baking pan that isn't warped, and rotate it halfway through baking.*

SALTINE
TOFFEE
BARK

||||||||||||||||||||||||||||||||||||

*These salty-sweet treasures
make delightful gifts, and their
flavor is simply irresistible.
The bark is like brittle, but
better. Get ready for a new
family favorite!*
—Laura Cox, South Dennis, MA

PREP: 15 MIN.
BAKE: 10 MIN. + CHILLING
MAKES: 2 LBS.

40	**saltines**
1	**cup butter, cubed**
¾	**cup sugar**
2	**cups semisweet chocolate chips**
1	**pkg. (8 oz.) milk chocolate English toffee bits**

1. Line a 15x10x1-in. baking pan with heavy-duty foil. Arrange saltines in a single layer on foil; set aside.

2. In a large heavy saucepan over medium heat, melt butter. Stir in sugar. Bring to a boil; cook and stir for 1-2 minutes or until sugar is dissolved. Pour evenly over crackers.

3. Bake at 350° for 8-10 minutes or until bubbly. Immediately sprinkle with chocolate chips. Allow chips to soften for a few minutes, then spread over top. Sprinkle with toffee bits. Cool.

4. Cover and refrigerate for 1 hour or until set. Break into pieces. Store in an airtight container.

||||||||||||

1 oz.: 171 cal., 12g fat (7g sat. fat), 21mg chol., 119mg sod., 18g carb. (11g sugars, 1g fiber), 1g pro.

> **Pump up the Flavor:** *For deeper, more nuanced flavors, substitute brown sugar for white or brown your butter before adding the sugar.*

ZUCCHINI
COBBLER

||||||||||||||||||||||||||||||||||

*This cobbler is my surprise
dessert! No one ever guesses
that the secret ingredient is
zucchini. Everyone says it
tastes like apples. It's fantastic
to make for a potluck supper
or to serve to a crowd.*
—Joanne Fazio, Carbondale, PA

PREP: 35 MIN.
BAKE: 35 MIN.
MAKES: 20 SERVINGS

- 8 **cups chopped seeded peeled zucchini (about 3 lbs. untrimmed)**
- ⅔ **cup lemon juice**
- 1 **cup sugar**
- 1 **tsp. ground cinnamon**
- ½ **tsp. ground nutmeg**

CRUST
- 4 **cups all-purpose flour**
- 2 **cups sugar**
- 1½ **cups cold butter, cubed**
- 1 **tsp. ground cinnamon**

1. Preheat oven to 375°. In a large saucepan over medium-low heat, cook and stir zucchini and lemon juice until zucchini is tender, 15-20 minutes. Stir in sugar, cinnamon and nutmeg; cook 1 minute longer. Remove from the heat; set aside.

2. In a large bowl, combine flour and sugar; cut in butter until mixture resembles coarse crumbs. Stir ½ cup into zucchini mixture. Press half the remaining crust mixture into a greased 15x10x1-in. baking pan. Spread the zucchini mixture over top; crumble remaining crust mixture over the zucchini. Sprinkle with cinnamon.

3. Bake until golden and bubbly, 35-40 minutes. Cool in pan on a wire rack.

||||||||||||

1 piece: 341 cal., 14g fat (9g sat. fat), 37mg chol., 114mg sod., 52g carb. (32g sugars, 1g fiber), 3g pro.

DR PEPPER SHEET CAKE

When we visited the Dr Pepper museum in Dublin, Texas, I bought a Dr Pepper cake mix. It was so delicious that I decided to create my own version. Here's the tasty result.
—Karen Daigle, Burleson, TX

PREP: 10 MIN.
BAKE: 20 MIN. + COOLING
MAKES: 24 SERVINGS

- 2 cups all-purpose flour
- 2 cups sugar
- 1 tsp. baking soda
- 1 tsp. ground cinnamon
- 2 cups Dr Pepper
- 1 cup butter, cubed
- ¼ cup baking cocoa
- 2 large eggs, room temperature, lightly beaten

ICING

- ½ cup butter, cubed
- ⅓ cup Dr Pepper
- ¼ cup baking cocoa
- 3¾ cups confectioners' sugar
- 1 tsp. ground cinnamon
- 1 tsp. vanilla extract
- 1 cup chopped pecans, toasted

1. Preheat oven to 350°. Grease a 15x10x1-in. baking pan. In a large bowl, whisk the flour, sugar, baking soda and cinnamon. In a small saucepan, combine Dr Pepper, butter and cocoa; bring just to a boil, stirring occasionally. Add to flour mixture, stirring just until moistened. Add eggs, whisking constantly.

2. Transfer to prepared pan, spreading evenly. Bake until a toothpick inserted in center comes out clean, 18-22 minutes.

3. Meanwhile, for icing, combine butter, Dr Pepper and cocoa in a small saucepan; stir over medium heat until smooth. Transfer to a bowl. Beat in confectioners' sugar, cinnamon and vanilla until smooth.

4. Remove cake from oven; place on a wire rack and let cool completely. Spread the frosting evenly over cake; sprinkle with pecans.

1 piece: 331 cal., 15g fat (8g sat. fat), 46mg chol., 154mg sod., 48g carb. (38g sugars, 1g fiber), 2g pro.

GIMLET
BARS

IIIIIIIIIIIIIIIIIIIIIIIIIIIIIIIIIII

I love a tangy gimlet when the weather turns steamy—but these bars are just the thing when the craving hits and summer seems too far away. Add more lime zest if you want these a bit tangier.
—Trisha Kruse, Eagle, ID

PREP: 20 MIN. + STANDING
BAKE: 35 MIN. + COOLING
MAKES: 4 DOZEN

   2   cups all-purpose flour
   ½   cup confectioners' sugar
   ½   tsp. salt
   1   cup butter

FILLING
   4   large eggs
   2   cups sugar
   ⅓   cup all-purpose flour
   ¼   cup lime juice
   ¼   cup gin
   1   Tbsp. grated lime zest
   ½   tsp. baking powder

GLAZE
   1½ cups confectioners'
        sugar
   2   Tbsp. lime juice
   2   Tbsp. gin
   1   tsp. grated lime zest

1. Preheat oven to 350°. Whisk flour, confectioners' sugar and salt; cut in butter until crumbly. Press onto the bottom of a greased 15x10x1-in. baking pan. Bake until golden brown, about 10 minutes. Cool on a wire rack.

2. For filling, whisk the 7 ingredients; spread over crust. Bake until filling is set, about 25 minutes. Cool completely in pan on a wire rack.

3. For glaze, whisk all ingredients until smooth; spread evenly over cooled bars. Let glaze set before serving.

IIIIIIIIIIIII

1 bar: 117 cal., 4g fat (3g sat. fat), 26mg chol., 66mg sod., 18g carb. (13g sugars, 0 fiber), 1g pro.

BLUEBERRY-BLACKBERRY
RUSTIC TART

IIIIIIIIIIIIIIIIIIIIIIIIIIIIIIIIIII

*My dad would always stop
our car on the side of the
road in Maine and say, "I
smell blueberries." He had a
pail ready. Then Mom would
bake the wild berries in a
cornmeal crust like this one.*
—Priscilla Gilbert, Indian Harbour Beach, FL

PREP: 20 MIN. + CHILLING
BAKE: 55 MIN.
MAKES: 8 SERVINGS

  2 **cups all-purpose flour**
  ⅓ **cup sugar**
  ¼ **cup yellow cornmeal**
  ⅔ **cup cold butter, cubed**
  ½ **cup buttermilk**

FILLING
  4 **cups fresh blueberries**
  2 **cups fresh blackberries**
  ⅔ **cup sugar**
  ⅓ **cup all-purpose flour**
  2 **Tbsp. lemon juice**
  1 **large egg, beaten**
  2 **Tbsp. turbinado
     (washed raw) sugar or
     coarse sugar
     Whipped cream,
     optional**

1. In a large bowl, mix flour, sugar and cornmeal; cut in butter until crumbly. Gradually add buttermilk, tossing with a fork until dough holds together when pressed. Shape into a disk; cover and refrigerate 30 minutes or overnight.

2. Preheat oven to 375°. On a lightly floured surface, roll dough into a 14-in. circle. Transfer to a parchment-lined baking sheet.

3. In a large bowl, combine berries, sugar, flour and lemon juice; spoon over the crust to within 2 in. of edge. Fold the crust edge over filling, leaving center uncovered. Brush folded crust with beaten egg; sprinkle with turbinado sugar.

4. Bake 55-60 minutes or until crust is golden brown and filling is bubbly. Using parchment, slide tart onto a wire rack to cool. If desired, serve with whipped cream.

IIIIIIIIIIII

*1 piece: 464 cal., 17g fat (10g sat. fat), 67mg chol.,
134mg sod., 74g carb. (38g sugars, 5g fiber), 7g pro.*

CHERRY
BARS

IIIIIIIIIIIIIIIIIIIIIIIIIIIIIIIII

Whip up a pan of these festive bars in just 20 minutes with staple ingredients and pie filling. Between the easy preparation and the pretty colors, they're destined to become a holiday classic.
—Jane Kamp, Grand Rapids, MI

PREP: 20 MIN.
BAKE: 35 MIN. + COOLING
MAKES: 5 DOZEN

- 1 **cup butter, softened**
- 2 **cups sugar**
- 1 **tsp. salt**
- 4 **large eggs,
     room temperature**
- 1 **tsp. vanilla extract**
- ¼ **tsp. almond extract**
- 3 **cups all-purpose flour**
- 2 **cans (21 oz. each)
     cherry pie filling**

GLAZE:
- 1 **cup confectioners' sugar**
- ½ **tsp. vanilla extract**
- ½ **tsp. almond extract**
- 2 **to 3 Tbsp. 2% milk**

1. Preheat oven to 350°. In a large bowl, cream butter, sugar and salt until light and fluffy, 5-7 minutes. Add eggs, 1 at a time, beating well after each addition. Beat in extracts. Gradually add flour.

2. Spread 3 cups dough into a greased 15x10x1-in. baking pan. Spread with pie filling. Drop remaining dough by teaspoonfuls over filling. Bake 35-40 minutes or until golden brown. Cool completely in pan on a wire rack.

3. In a small bowl, mix confectioners' sugar, extracts and enough milk to reach desired consistency; drizzle over top.

IIIIIIIIIIII

1 bar: 112 cal., 3g fat (2g sat. fat), 21mg chol., 72mg sod., 19g carb. (9g sugars, 0 fiber), 1g pro.

> *Switch It Up: Blueberry, apricot or raspberry pie filling works well in these bars. For a Black Forest variation, add a handful of mini chocolate chips to the dough.*

ROASTED STRAWBERRY
SHEET CAKE

||||||||||||||||||||||||||||||||

My Grandma Gigi just loved summer berry cakes. Almost any time I'd call her during the warmer months, she'd invite me over to taste her latest masterpiece. This sheet cake is an ode to her.
—Kristin Bowers, Rancho Palos Verdes, CA

PREP: 1 HOUR
BAKE: 30 MIN. + COOLING
MAKES: 24 SERVINGS

  4 **lbs. halved fresh strawberries**
  ½ **cup sugar**

CAKE
  1 **cup butter, softened**
 1½ **cups sugar**
  2 **large eggs, room temperature**
  2 **tsp. almond extract**
  3 **cups all-purpose flour**
  3 **tsp. baking powder**
  2 **tsp. salt**
  1 **cup 2% milk**
  ¼ **cup turbinado (washed raw) sugar**

1. Preheat oven to 350°. Place strawberries on a parchment-lined rimmed baking sheet. Sprinkle with sugar and toss to coat. Bake until just tender, 35-40 minutes. Cool slightly.

2. Meanwhile, grease a 15x10x1-in. baking pan. In a large bowl, cream butter and sugar until light and fluffy, 5-7 minutes. Add eggs, 1 at a time, beating well after each addition. Beat in the extract. In another bowl, whisk flour, baking powder and salt; add to creamed mixture alternately with milk, beating well after each addition (batter may appear curdled).

3. Transfer to the prepared pan. Top with 3 cups roasted strawberries; sprinkle with the turbinado sugar. Reserve remaining strawberries for serving. Bake until a toothpick inserted in center comes out clean, 30-35 minutes. Cool completely in pan on a wire rack. Serve the cake with reserved roasted strawberries.

|||||||||||

1 piece: 235 cal., 9g fat (5g sat. fat), 37mg chol., 329mg sod., 37g carb. (23g sugars, 2g fiber), 3g pro.

Sheet-Pan Secret: *When roasting the strawberries, it is important to use a rimmed baking sheet to capture all the juices that will be released.*

GRAPEFRUIT
ALASKA

||||||||||||||||||||||||||||||||||||

*Easily impress your guests
with this quick dessert. It
takes just 30 minutes to
prepare, and you'll receive
rave reviews.*
—Peg Atzen, Hackensack, MN

TAKES: 30 MIN.
MAKES: 8 SERVINGS

- 4 **large grapefruit**
- 2 **tsp. rum extract**
- ½ **cup heavy
  whipping cream,
  whipped**
- 3 **large egg whites,
  room temperature**
- 1 **tsp. cornstarch**
- ¼ **tsp. cream of tartar**
- ¼ **cup sugar**
- 8 **maraschino cherries**

1. Halve grapefruits and section; remove membranes. Return grapefruit sections to grapefruit halves. Drizzle ¼ tsp. rum extract over each. Top each with 1 rounded Tbsp. of whipped cream. Place on an ungreased foil-lined baking sheet.

2. In a large bowl, beat the egg whites, cornstarch and cream of tartar on medium speed until soft peaks form. Gradually beat in the sugar, 1 Tbsp. at a time, on high until stiff glossy peaks form and sugar is dissolved. Mound ½ cup on each grapefruit half; spread meringue to edges to seal. Bake at 350° until the meringue is browned, 15 minutes. Top each with a cherry. Serve immediately.

|||||||||||||

*½ grapefruit: 152 cal., 6g fat (3g sat. fat), 20mg chol.,
26mg sod., 24g carb. (21g sugars, 2g fiber), 3g pro.*

RASPBERRY
ALMOND
STRIPS

||||||||||||||||||||||||||||||||||

A cup of tea is the perfect complement to these scrumptious cookie strips. Dressed up with raspberry filling, the crunchy bites also include chopped almonds for an extra-special treat.
—*Taste of Home* Test Kitchen

PREP: 20 MIN.
BAKE: 15 MIN./BATCH
MAKES: 32 COOKIES

1   tube (16½ oz.) refrigerated sugar cookie dough, softened
⅔   cup all-purpose flour
½   cup finely chopped almonds
6   Tbsp. raspberry cake and pastry filling

1. Preheat oven to 350°. In a bowl, beat the cookie dough, flour and almonds until blended. Divide dough in half. Roll each half into a 13½x2-in. rectangle on an ungreased baking sheet.

2. Using a wooden spoon handle, make a ¼-in.-deep indentation lengthwise down the center of each rectangle. Bake 5 minutes.

3. Spoon raspberry filling into indentation. Bake 8-10 minutes longer or until cookie is golden brown. Cool on pans 2 minutes.

4. Remove from pans to a cutting board; cut each rectangle crosswise into 16 slices. Transfer to wire racks to cool.

|||||||||||||

1 cookie: 106 cal., 4g fat (1g sat. fat), 2mg chol., 55mg sod., 16g carb. (9g sugars, 1g fiber), 1g pro.

BUTTERMILK
BLUEBERRY SCOOKIES

IIIIIIIIIIIIIIIIIIIIIIIIIIIIIIIIIIIIII

The idea for "scookies" was born after I made cookie shapes out of scone dough. Light and crispy right from the oven, they're just sweet enough to enjoy at any time of the day.

—Ally Phillips, Murrells Inlet, SC

TAKES: 25 MIN.
MAKES: 12 COOKIES

- 2 cups all-purpose flour
- ½ cup plus 1 Tbsp. sugar, divided
- 2 tsp. baking powder
- 1 tsp. baking soda
- ½ cup cold butter, cubed
- ½ cup buttermilk
- 1 large egg, room temperature, lightly beaten
- 1 cup fresh or frozen blueberries, thawed

1. Preheat oven to 375°. In a large bowl, whisk flour, ½ cup sugar, baking powder and baking soda. Cut in butter until mixture resembles coarse crumbs. In another bowl, whisk buttermilk and egg until blended; stir into crumb mixture just until moistened.

2. Drop dough by scant ¼ cupfuls 2 in. apart onto a parchment-lined baking sheet. Form a ½-in.-deep indentation in center of each with the back of a spoon coated with cooking spray. Gently press blueberries into the indentations; sprinkle with the remaining sugar.

3. Bake until golden brown, 11-14 minutes. Serve warm.

IIIIIIIIIIIII

1 cookie: 197 cal., 8g fat (5g sat. fat), 36mg chol., 258mg sod., 28g carb. (11g sugars, 1g fiber), 3g pro.

BROWNIE
TORTE

|||||||||||||||||||||||||||||||||||||

*My mother-in-law first shared
this recipe, and now it's often
requested for birthdays and
other special occasions. I like to
serve it at Christmastime on an
antique platter surrounded by
ornaments for decoration.*
—Candace McClure, Brookville, IN

PREP: 30 MIN.
BAKE: 15 MIN. + COOLING
MAKES: 12 SERVINGS

- 1 cup miniature
   semisweet
   chocolate chips
- ⅔ cup butter, cubed
- 4 large eggs,
   room temperature
- 1½ cups sugar
- 1½ cups all-purpose flour
- 1 tsp. baking powder
- ½ tsp. salt
- ½ cup coarsely chopped
   walnuts

FROSTING
- 2 cups heavy
   whipping cream
- ¼ cup confectioners' sugar
- 1 tsp. vanilla extract
- 1 cup miniature
   semisweet
   chocolate chips
   Additional
   miniature semisweet
   chocolate chips, optional

1. Preheat oven to 350°. Line a 15x10x1-in. baking pan with
parchment.

2. In a microwave, melt chocolate chips and butter; stir until
smooth. Cool slightly. In a large bowl, beat eggs and sugar. Stir
in chocolate mixture. In another bowl, mix flour, baking powder
and salt; gradually add to chocolate mixture, mixing well. Fold
in the walnuts.

3. Transfer to prepared pan. Bake 15-20 minutes or until
a toothpick inserted in the center comes out clean (do not
overbake). Cool 10 minutes. Invert onto a flat surface dusted
with confectioners' sugar. Gently peel off the parchment.
Cool completely.

4. In a bowl, beat cream, confectioners' sugar and vanilla until
stiff peaks form. Fold in chocolate chips. Trim cake edges; cut
crosswise into fourths. Place 1 layer on a serving plate; top
with ¾ cup frosting. Repeat twice. Top with the remaining
layer. Frost top, sides and ends of cake. If desired, sprinkle
with additional chocolate chips. Store in the refrigerator.

||||||||||||

*1 slice: 586 cal., 38g fat (22g sat. fat), 134mg chol.,
258mg sod., 60g carb. (45g sugars, 2g fiber), 7g pro.*

PUMPKIN
BARS

||||||||||||||||||||||||||||||||||||||

*What could be a better
fall treat than a big pan of
pumpkin-flavored bars?
Actually, my family loves
these any time of year,
and I bet yours will, too!*
—Brenda Keller, Andalusia, AL

PREP: 20 MIN.
BAKE: 25 MIN. + COOLING
MAKES: 2 DOZEN

  4 **large eggs,
      room temperature**
1⅔ **cups sugar**
  1 **cup canola oil**
  1 **can (15 oz.) pumpkin**
  2 **cups all-purpose flour**
  2 **tsp. ground cinnamon**
  2 **tsp. baking powder**
  1 **tsp. baking soda**
  1 **tsp. salt**

ICING
  6 **oz. cream cheese,
      softened**
  2 **cups confectioners'
      sugar**
 ¼ **cup butter, softened**
  1 **tsp. vanilla extract**
  1 **to 2 Tbsp. 2% milk**

1. In a bowl, beat the eggs, sugar, oil and pumpkin until well blended. Combine the flour, cinnamon, baking powder, baking soda and salt; gradually add to pumpkin mixture and mix well. Pour into an ungreased 15x10x1-in. baking pan. Bake at 350° for 25-30 minutes or until set. Cool completely.

2. For the icing, beat the cream cheese, confectioners' sugar, butter and vanilla in a small bowl. Add enough milk to achieve spreading consistency. Spread icing over bars. Store the bars in the refrigerator.

||||||||||||||

*1 bar: 260 cal., 13g fat (3g sat. fat), 45mg chol.,
226mg sod., 34g carb. (24g sugars, 1g fiber), 3g pro.*

APPLE RED-HOT
SLAB PIE

||||||||||||||||||||||||||||||||||||

This dessert is my family's absolute favorite because it holds so many memories for us. Red Hots give the filling a color that makes it an instant hit at parties.
—Linda Morten, Somerville, TX

PREP: 45 MIN. + CHILLING
BAKE: 50 MIN.
MAKES: 24 SERVINGS

5   cups all-purpose flour
2   Tbsp. sugar
2   tsp. salt
2   cups cold butter, cubed
1   to 1¼ cups ice water

FILLING
⅔   cup sugar
⅔   cup all-purpose flour
½   tsp. salt
6   cups thinly sliced peeled
     Granny Smith apples
     (about 6 medium)
6   cups thinly sliced peeled
     Gala or Jonathan apples
     (about 6 medium)
1   cup Red Hots candies
¼   cup cold butter
     Vanilla ice cream,
     optional

1. In a large bowl, mix flour, sugar and salt; cut in butter until crumbly. Gradually add ice water, tossing with a fork until dough holds together when pressed. Divide the dough into 2 portions so that 1 portion is slightly larger than the other. Shape each into a rectangle; cover and refrigerate 1 hour or overnight.

2. Preheat oven to 375°. For filling, in a large bowl, mix sugar, flour and salt. Add apples and Red Hots; toss to coat.

3. On a lightly floured surface, roll out larger portion of dough into an 18x13-in. rectangle. Transfer to ungreased 15x10x1-in. baking pan. Press onto the bottom and up the sides of pan. Add filling; dot with butter.

4. Roll out remaining dough; place over filling. Fold bottom crust over edge of top crust; seal and flute or press with a fork to seal. Prick top with a fork.

5. Bake 50-55 minutes or until golden brown and filling is bubbly. Cool on a wire rack. Serve warm. If desired, serve with ice cream.

||||||||||||

1 piece: 349 cal., 18g fat (11g sat. fat), 46mg chol., 383mg sod., 45g carb. (19g sugars, 2g fiber), 3g pro.

PEANUT BUTTER
SHEET CAKE

||||||||||||||||||||||||||||||||||||

I received this recipe from a minister's wife, and my family just loves it.
—Brenda Jackson, Garden City, KS

PREP: 15 MIN.
BAKE: 20 MIN. + COOLING
MAKES: 24 SERVINGS

- 2 cups all-purpose flour
- 2 cups sugar
- 1 tsp. baking soda
- ½ tsp. salt
- 1 cup water
- ¾ cup butter, cubed
- ½ cup chunky peanut butter
- ¼ cup canola oil
- 2 large eggs, room temperature
- ½ cup buttermilk
- 1 tsp. vanilla extract

GLAZE
- ⅔ cup sugar
- ⅓ cup evaporated milk
- 1 Tbsp. butter
- ⅓ cup chunky peanut butter
- ⅓ cup miniature marshmallows
- ½ tsp. vanilla extract

1. Preheat oven to 350°. Grease a 15x10x1-in. baking pan.

2. In a large bowl, whisk flour, sugar, baking soda and salt. In a small saucepan, combine water and butter; bring just to a boil. Stir in peanut butter and oil until blended. Stir into flour mixture. In a small bowl, whisk eggs, buttermilk and vanilla until blended; add to flour mixture, whisking constantly.

3. Transfer to prepared pan. Bake until a toothpick inserted in center comes out clean, 20-25 minutes.

4. Meanwhile, for glaze, combine sugar, milk and butter in a saucepan. Bring to a boil, stirring constantly; cook and stir 2 minutes. Remove from heat; stir in the peanut butter, marshmallows and vanilla until blended. Spoon over the warm cake, spreading evenly. Cool on a wire rack.

|||||||||||||

1 piece: 266 cal., 14g fat (5g sat. fat), 36mg chol., 222mg sod., 33g carb. (23g sugars, 1g fiber), 4g pro.

READER REVIEW
"I made this for my husband's poker night and it was a hit with the guys. They compared it to a peanut butter cup. I did add ¾ cup chocolate chips to the icing."
—PDARWIN, TASTEOFHOME.COM

RECEIPE
INDEX

IIIIIIIIIIIIIIIIIIII